Sherri Falco's *The Giving Tree: Beyond Nominal Christianity* is an engaging, exciting read that touches the heart, builds faith, and clarifies theological issues. Dr. Sherri Falco has a doctorate in Juris Prudence, J.D. and a doctorate in Ministry, D.Min. She has lived upon the mountaintop of the American success dream and walked through the valley of loss, despair, and hopelessness—until she discovered hope, faith, and love. Her personal story is so interesting that it is hard to put the book down. I don't want to give away the true storyline; just get the book and read it—you will be glad I recommended it to you.

— **Dr. Randy Clark**
Overseer of the apostolic network of Global Awakening
President of Global Awakening Theological Seminary

The Giving Tree by Dr. Sherri Falco is a prophetic challenge to contemporary American Christianity which has compartmentalized the ministry of caring for the poor and afflicted in our society and the ministry of the power of the Holy Spirit that the early church experienced in advancing the Gospel of the kingdom of God. Sherri's powerful testimony of the leading of the Holy Spirit into the ministry of the Giving Tree and the incredible miracles of healing, provision, and deliverance experienced by those receiving their ministry is a wonderful adventure into the heart of God for humanity. This book is an antidote for discouragement in the midst of faithful service. It is my privilege to recommend this book to you from my friend.

— **Dr. Mike Hutchings**
Director of Education, Global Awakening
President and Founder, God Heals PTSD Foundation
Author of *Supernatural Freedom from Captivity to Trauma: Overcoming the Hindrance to your Wholeness*

THE
Giving Tree

Beyond Nominal Christianity

Sherri L. Falco, JD, DMin

The Giving Tree: Beyond Nominal Christianity
Copyright © 2021 by Sherri L. Falco

Published by Eyes Open Press
West Milford, New Jersey
Visit us at www.EyesOpenPress.com

No part of this book may be reproduced without written permission from the publisher or copyright holder, nor may any part of this book be transmitted in any form or by any means electronic, mechanical, photocopying, recording, or other, without prior written permission from the publisher or copyright holder.

Unless otherwise indicated, all Scripture quotations are taken from the Holy Bible, NEW INTERNATIONAL VERSION®, NIV® Copyright © 1973, 1978, 1984, 2011 by Biblica, Inc.® Used by permission. All rights reserved worldwide.

Scripture quotations marked ESV are from the ESV® Bible (The Holy Bible, English Standard Version®), copyright © 2001 by Crossway, a publishing ministry of Good News Publishers. Used by permission. All rights reserved.

Library of Congress Control Number: 2021913911

ISBNs: 978-1-7360733-3-9 (Print)
        978-1-7360733-4-6 (E-book)

Printed in the United States of America.

Abba, this is all for you.

Acknowledgments

I wish to express my sincerest gratitude to my family for their love and support. My two sons, Christopher and Zachary, you are my treasures from heaven, my inspiration, and a living testimony to the love and miraculous power of God. You make my heart sing.

My husband, Pasquale, you are a living example of what it means to be a disciple of Jesus Christ. You have taught me to cling to the simplicity of the gospel and are most definitely the Lord's best for me.

I am also grateful to my sisters in Christ, Sue Wexler and Allison Lee, whose true friendship has made all of this possible, and to Tom Litteer, Jon Ruthven, and Andrew Park, whose wisdom and mentoring have been invaluable.

Contents

Foreword		13
Introduction		15
1	Becoming Abba's Child	19
2	The Faith Experience	33
3	Encountering Christ	49
4	Transformed by Love	67
5	Called to Be a Witness	85
6	Sound	111
7	Grace Notes from Heaven	131
8	A New Song for the Bride	161
Epilogue		207

"Father, where shall I work today?"

And my love flowed warm and free.

Then he pointed me out a tiny spot,

And said, "Tend that for me."

I answered quickly, "Oh, no, not that.

Why, no one would ever see,

No matter how well my work was done.

Not that little place for me!"

And the word he spoke, it was not stern,

He answered me tenderly,

"Ah, little one, search that heart of thine;

Art thou working for them or me?

Nazareth was a little place,

And so was Galilee."

—*Author unknown*

Foreword

Traditional Christianity has mostly avoided, even denied, its origins in the power of God as a model for what should have continued in the church. Dr. Falco's new book returns the church to its authentic, original pattern. This work represents a breakthrough expression of how the gospel is "fulfilled" (Romans 15:19 ESV) in the New Testament, that is, "in word and deed" [prophecy and miracle] "By the power of signs and wonders, by the power of the Spirit . . . *fulfilled* the ministry of the gospel."

Dr. Falco's book shows this fundamental understanding of St. Paul of the central nature of the gospel itself: "The kingdom of God is not a matter of talk [theology and creeds] but of power" (1 Corinthians 4:20). Hence, this work—fully expressed in a ministry of miraculous healings and provisions faithful to these New Testament principles—is actually more "biblical" than the traditional orthodoxy it challenges!

Throughout this book, Dr. Falco lays out the redeeming and loving power of God in action through an examination of the book of Ruth and other scriptures, and through the powerful ministry of healing and miracles that God has bestowed upon this writer of *The Giving Tree: Beyond Nominal Christianity*. This is a must-read for anyone interested in the authentic, original Christianity of Jesus.

— **Jon Ruthven**, PhD, Director, PhD Program, Iris University
Author of *What's Wrong with Protestant Theology: Tradition vs. Biblical Emphasis*.

Introduction

The inspiration for this book arose out of my conversion experience, which was accompanied by a powerful baptism of the Holy Spirit and induction into the ranks of the children of God who hear his voice and respond in faith. I was summarily set on my feet and sent out to pray for healing. I listened to God, spoke what I heard, and miracles followed.

I learned what it means to be a child of God; a child of faith who worships the Father in spirit and in truth. A child of God is one who hears the voice of God and responds appropriately. Every child of God was created to release the glory of God by being "sounded." That is the "Christ in you, the hope of glory." In other words, the Holy Spirit within the believer is the potential for releasing God's power on the earth through the spoken word. This is at the heart of what it means to be created in the image of God. God's sound is the answer to the question of identity because it addresses the questions "who am I?" and "who is God?"

The sound of God that takes up residence in the believer holds the potential to release heaven on earth when it is in harmony with heaven, reflecting both love and humility. When we redefine our purpose as being someone who releases the Father's love song wherever we go, it will lift the burden of striving and silence the voice of religion. The simple job description of every believer is to listen to the Holy Spirit, see what he sees, and say what he says. It is crucial for us to hear the voice of God because it allows us to see from heaven's vantage point. This heavenly discernment enables us to see what God sees and then love as God loves in every situation. Only then will the sound that is released through our lives harmonize with heaven.

There is great value in the "little things," for value is inherent in the kingdom of God. God greatly enjoys pouring his power and favor on the unlikely, the people deemed worthless and unusable, and in places humans would never choose. God loves to answer Nathanael's question with a resounding yes: "Nazareth! Can anything good come from there?" (John 1:46). In God's kingdom, no one is excluded from the offer to have a voice and to "be sounded" for his glory, as well as the offer to live as a child of God and enjoy the new covenant relationship.

The exploration of the power of sound—particularly of the spoken word and in releasing God's kingdom here on earth—has been the defining characteristic of my journey as a disciple of Christ. While an exhaustive theology of sound is outside the present scope of this book, the following establishes a biblical basis for the power of the spoken word as the primary avenue for the release of God's kingdom here on earth. This foundation, combined with thirteen years of the real-world "missions" experience of Giving Tree (consisting of eyewitness testimonies of the miraculous in the lives of ordinary people in New England and New York), establishes the basis for a replicable biblical paradigm for discipleship. On a much larger scale, it is my heart's desire that this book will contribute to a much-needed paradigm shift both for the individual believer and for the church as a whole.

To be a disciple of Christ is synonymous with being a witness for Christ. A witness, in turn, is one who has firsthand experience with the action of God and gives a verbal account of it. At the very center of the journey with Christ and at the heart of discipleship lies faith. The emphasis of this book and the target at which it is squarely aimed is the issue of faith. Faith is, was, and always has been the primary requirement for the child of God. Jesus sent his disciples out to proclaim the kingdom, heal the sick, and drive out demons. He sent them out on an

Introduction

impossible mission and instructed them to take nothing with them. It was the presence of Jesus Christ through the Holy Spirit ensuring that the impossible would become possible. This is the essence of faith. It is the sound of what it means to "live not by bread alone, but on every word that comes from the mouth of God."

Nominal Christianity declares that faith is "optional"—biblical Christianity states otherwise. The absence of faith renders the sound of God impossible. The sound of God is the sound of Psalm 23. It is the sound of the Holy Spirit speaking through David, declaring, "The Lord is my shepherd. I shall lack nothing." The sound of faith declares, "God is enough." It is the sound of heaven becoming an orchestra on earth through the symphony of believers. It is the keynote of Giving Tree, and the impetus behind the paradigm shift.

1

Becoming Abba's Child

The Narrow Road to Bethlehem

Your name is Ruth," said the Lord after a powerful yet unsolicited baptism of the Holy Spirit. Having traveled for decades down the path of least resistance far into dark places, God, by his grace, brought me home.

> *Two roads diverged in a wood, and I—*
> *I took the one less traveled by,*
> *And that has made all the difference.*
> — Robert Frost[1]

That Christmas Eve, my mother silently watched my father pack his belongings. My sister was unintelligible beneath her sobs. Until that year, Christmas was greatly anticipated, and the world was good. Wasn't the very existence of Santa Claus who showered gifts on every child proof that the world was good? Something broke inside me that day as my father prepared to leave us for his "other family," which, unbeknownst to us, he had cultivated for five years. My stony-faced mother had to pry me off the tailgate of my father's truck so he could

---
1. Robert Frost, "The Road Not Taken," *Mountain Interval* (Henry Holt and Company: New York, 1916).

The Giving Tree

leave. My father left, and life was never the same. Every little girl wants to believe in a fairytale. At nine years old, Santa Claus was no longer real, and the world was no longer good.

My father was very vocal about his desire for sons and his deep disappointment that he had daughters. From the outset, the message was that girls were inferior. They were God's second choice, both second-rate and second-best. The first four decades of my life were spent trying to prove otherwise. My walls were covered with tokens of my achievements and benchmarks of the road to success. The broad road that leads to worldly success is a world of measurement, both linear and predictable, where personal worth is measured by the size of one's bank account, by the power one wields, and the popularity one enjoys. All of these are indicators of significance in the world. The problem, however, is that the void in the quest for significance is God-shaped and can never be filled with anything else.

> Enter through the narrow gate. For wide is the gate and broad is the road that leads to destruction, and many enter through it. But small is the gate and narrow the road that leads to life, and only a few find it. (Matthew 7:13-14)

After climbing rung after rung up the illusory ladder of success, all my energy was spent. As the door closed behind me concluding my last day at one of the most prestigious law firms in New York City, for the first time in my life there were no plans for the future, no next step, and no goal in mind. In that quietness of soul surfaced the deep desire to have children. A small peek into the vastness of the universe hints that a full understanding of its Creator is not within human reach. Any woman who has experienced the unparalleled pain of infertility can attest to this truth. The desire to have children is God-given, so when God chooses to delay or even deny that desire, an indescribable struggle begins in a woman's soul. Infertility is a type of death sentence for women. Infertile women experience depression at rates indistinguishable from those of women with cancer, heart disease, hypertension, and HIV.[2] After three years of trying to conceive and undergoing a multitude of unsuccessful procedures, the last battery of tests had been performed, and the verdict was in: the odds of motherhood for me were less than ten percent. My husband was exonerated from any fault, and the death knell of unexplained infertility was lowered on my life. The blame for our childlessness was mine and mine alone.

Childbearing, a fact to which Hannah, Rachel, Sarah, and many of the Bible's matriarchs can attest, is the one activity in which we cannot engage without God. Procreation and life are relegated exclusively to the realm of God and are done by his power. There are no imitations and no substitutes. No amount of striving or cleverly invented medical intervention is of any value without God's active participation. God alone is the giver of life. For the first time in my life, all of my efforts were futile apart from God. The bitter and angry person staring back at me from the mirror each morning was unrecognizable. My medical options had not run out, but exhaustion and hopelessness had set in. Deciding to discontinue all treatment and to trust God alone was one of the most difficult decisions of my life. My friends and family were incredulous. Surely this was not serious. Their voices echoed the very doubt that was my constant struggle: *What if God doesn't come for you?*

There were dozens of reasons God could choose to punish me. Perhaps my infertility was a justly deserved divine retribution. Cowering in shame, my prayer was simple: "Lord, you alone are the giver of all life. If you want me to be a mother, it's in your hands." He answered with a vision of me returning a child to him. The vision seemed a bit backward, after all, since there was no child to give back, but my interpretation was that all children are his. One year later, unaided by human hands, my first child, Christopher, was born. Two years later would usher in the birth of my second child, Zachary. Maybe God loved me after all?

---

2. Alice D. Domar, Ph.D.and Henry Dreher, *Healing Mind, Healthy Woman: Using the Mind-Body Connection to Manage Stress and Take Control of Your Life* (New York: Henry Holt and Company, 1997), 233.

The Giving Tree

Abba's Child

The voice of the prestigious Greenwich company's CEO faded into white noise as he listed all of the reasons why their offer of employment was so compelling. My attention was elsewhere. Requesting a break in the middle of an interview was unprecedented, and the CEO looked puzzled at my sudden need to place an urgent phone call. My four-month-old son was with a babysitter, and my neglect to inform her about his intense dislike for peas had been circling in my brain for the duration of the interview. The situation needed to be rectified. This was the definitive moment when the profound change in me became apparent. Gone was the overachieving lawyer—she had been replaced by a mother.

Arriving home, I broke the news of my intention not to return to work to my husband, who had for months been piling job openings into my lap to ensure the satisfaction of my share of the financial burden. Another human being had never been completely dependent upon me for his well-being, so, contrary to my husband's wishes, the unthinkable had happened. I had chosen to "just" be a mother. That day my marriage died. Until my husband filed for divorce ten years later, another soul never learned my secret. The price of depriving my Russian-born husband of his American dream, which included a Harvard-trained lawyer as a wife and a commensurate earning potential, was his love. To onlookers, our family was idyllic. Ten years of my life were spent in silence as a single mother, a widow with a living husband. Out of outsiders' view, my husband withdrew from the children and me, taking his love with him. Completely ignored, my role was a non-person without any value or significance. My petitions for counseling and help to save our marriage were met with a cold, steadfast refusal. As a nominal Christian with limited knowledge of Scripture, divorce was never an option because "God hates divorce" (see Malachi 2:16).

Unaware that a relationship with God was a possibility and with no real outlet for the pain, my decision was simply not to care. Having officially entered the ranks of the walking dead, my search for God began in bitterness and anger. No one was there to guide me on how or where to find God. Logically, one should be able to find God in church, right? My search extended from church to church and denomination to denomination but ended in a land of confusion. Religion was everywhere, but God was not. If God was not in the church, then perhaps he could be found in a seminary where pastors are trained, was my reasoning. Yet God was not to be found in seminary either. Repeatedly, my cry to heaven was a question that hung unanswered in the air, "God, where are you?"

In January 2007, an obscure class called Divine Healing appeared on the seminary schedule. The title was intriguing, and I enrolled. It was my custom to arrive early for a bit of quiet time before class began. The first day, much to my displeasure, the room was already occupied by two women who immediately addressed me upon my arrival. "We prayed for a divine appointment," one of them explained. "It must be you." Puzzled at what a "divine appointment" might be and not at all certain it was desirable, an uncomfortable silence ensued. Sensing my bewilderment, they explained they wanted to pray for me.

Rather than drawing near to me, they stood at quite a distance because, they claimed, "God had instructed them to do so." My first thought was God didn't want them to catch something undesirable from me. My mind was racing with the various possibilities of what that "something" might be when one of them said three simple words: *"Come, Holy Spirit."* Waves of liquid love washed over me in that moment. All of my false beliefs about God dissolved in an instant. He was not distant and angry. Undone and sobbing, the realization descended upon me—God was not only real; he cared. Even more, he was here.

"Your name is Ruth," the Lord said with crystal clear clarity. In the blink of an eye, I was resurrected from the ranks of the walking dead, was put on my feet, given a new name, and instructed to pray for healing. Cancer was healed. Cystic fibrosis was healed. Paralytics walked in the name of Jesus, and blind eyes were opened. Miracles, signs, and wonders broke out everywhere.

The Giving Tree

My hope in the fairytale had revived, and I forged ahead with bright hopes for the future, completely unaware of the opposition that would arise within my own family. Initially, my husband was irritated at my continued willingness to pray for strangers. That irritation subsided temporarily as he contemplated the potentially lucrative nature of miracles. "How much do you think someone would pay for a miracle?" he asked. My response was simple but definitive. "Jesus' healing was, is, and always will be free. It is God's grace made manifest. It is a gift." In time, many male voices would rise up in the church in opposition to render a verdict of guilty for me as an unsubmissive wife.

The church had become a weapon in the hands of my husband. God himself became the ultimate weapon of choice. Word of the miracles started to spread, and invitations to pray for the sick came from increasingly distant places. Suddenly and inexplicably, doors began to close. Having spent years withdrawn in silence, keeping the troubles in my marriage a secret, I was hurled to the forefront of a frenzy of unfounded accusations leveled at me by fellow Christians. They questioned the source of the power for the miracles, my character, and my identity. The most painful aspect of it all was that my own husband started the spark that had ignited the wildfire.

The short-lived fairytale had come to an abrupt end. My prince had not come, and I was not Abba's child. My husband had testified to my lack of worth, value, and significance, and apparently God agreed. If God was truly against me, as my husband claimed, then truly no one was for me. Throughout all of it, voices repeatedly judged me, my marriage, and my relationship with God. As they put it, my only salvation was to turn around, go back, and submit to my husband.

In a secular courtroom, one is innocent until proven guilty, and in all circumstances, the accused is allowed to speak in his or her own defense. Shockingly the legal standard in the church was not only lower—it was the complete opposite: guilty until proven innocent. This was an uphill battle that cannot be won. The world was not good, and the world was in the church.

Becoming Abba's Child

My choice to follow God had led me into a land of confusion. In the church, my husband's behavior was that of an exemplary Christian. Ironically, the only one unaware of his purported conversion was me. Late one night, while taking out the garbage and with his back toward me, my husband casually announced he had filed for divorce. The battle lines were drawn. My husband had liquidated most of the marital assets in anticipation of the divorce, and my name was simply removed from the remainder. My status was downgraded to "nonexistent." Without any source of income and no means of support, my path led into the ranks of the destitute. My faith was now to be put on trial in the secular courtroom.

My husband assembled a noteworthy legal team whose singular goal was to prove, rather ironically, that I was an unfit mother. Accused of hearing voices, my private papers were put on parade and even ridiculed by court officials. My Harvard Law degree was useless, as proving the absence of something is quite impossible. How does one prove that he or she does not hear voices? How does one prove that the Holy Spirit is not one of the undesirable voices to be heard? My husband ridiculed my faith, saying, "What if God does not come for you?" The despair from the battle over my children would have caused me to turn back had it been possible. This Ruth, however, was far from Moab and well on the way to Bethlehem. There was no way to turn back. God was very silent then, but not still. He used two women to deliver me from the confusion and to stand me back up; one a devout Christian, the other, an avowed atheist. Leave it to God to use women.

The first woman God chose was Heidi Baker of Iris Ministries. Haunted by all the terrible things that my husband attributed to me, the jury was still out as to the question of my identity. At a conference in Long Island, Heidi came down off the stage and walked right past me. As a nonperson, being ignored was expected. Then Heidi did the unthinkable. Not turning around, she deliberately walked backward and knelt down right in front of me. Taking me in her arms, she rocked me for an eternity. Hundreds of people were waiting for ministry, but Heidi

The Giving Tree

was in no hurry. She simply held me and whispered something into my hair while I cried. Maybe, just maybe, I was God's child after all.

"You and I are not on the same page," announced the court-appointed psychologist. "I do not believe in your God." All hope evaporated. The court had appointed a psychologist to investigate my husband's allegations and evaluate my fitness as a parent. Session after session and hour after hour, the psychologist evaluated my husband, my children, and me. This continued for almost a year as the drama played out in the courtroom. Then a meeting was called. She had made her diagnosis. Standing in front of a group of five men and me, she said, "The husband is not who you think he is, and the wife is not who you think she is. You have it backward."

A wave of relief washed over me as suddenly the scales shifted in my favor. As she presented her diagnosis, an invisible burden was lifted. My husband had a disorder called Narcissistic Personality Disorder, which involves pathological lying and what psychologists term stealth abuse. The narcissist rarely uses outright physical violence, which leaves telltale signs, but sets out a more covert course to methodically destroy the victim's identity. God used this woman to bring me home. Yes, God can even use an atheist!

Ruth was a barren, destitute widow, a foreigner who chose to follow Yahweh, a God she did not know. She stood at a crossroads and decided not to go back to Moab or its gods but to commit herself instead to living as a child of God. Ruth's culture gave her no voice, no status, and no worth. Her circumstances testified to the fact that she was nothing. Ruth was insignificant to her world. Thankfully, God had quite a different idea. Hundreds of years before the birth of Jesus, God put his plan for redemption in place, and he used a woman, a barren foreign widow. God chose Ruth. Not only does God specialize in lost causes, but he loves to use them to do great things.

My entire journey has been a search for my identity as Abba's child. I have wrestled with God, questioned him, doubted, and gone astray.

Becoming Abba's Child

He has been there all along, though, watching over me and showering me with traces of his grace. Risk, self-sacrifice, and pain have been an unavoidable part of the journey and arguably necessary. Through it all, he has taught me to fight in the opposite spirit, to forgive daily, and to not value titles, signs and wonders, or empty words, but fruit that demonstrates the character and heart of God.

The true test of faith and the journey to significance lies in our daily life. Personal value, significance, and ultimately identity come under assault when daily circumstances mount up as negative evidence. Don't we all want God to come for us in the nitty-gritty moments of our lives and declare that he is, indeed, Abba?

The invitation of the death and resurrection of Jesus Christ that would happen centuries after Ruth is an invitation into a relationship. It is an invitation to be Abba's child. What does it mean to be a child of God?

> For those who are led by the Spirit of God are the children of God. The Spirit you received does not make you slaves, so that you live in fear again; rather, the Spirit you received brought about your adoption to sonship. And by him we cry, "Abba, Father." (Romans 8:14-15)

Loving God Enough to Break the Rules

Our world has a scarcity mindset where competition is key. It is a zero-sum game where, in order for me to win, you must lose. This is a world without grace, without relationship, self-focused instead of God-focused, where everything is linear and predictable, measured and compared. In contrast, the kingdom of God is a non-zero-sum game where the whole is greater than the sum of the parts, and where the only way to have more is to give everything away. It is a world where the greatest is the least, where the way up is down. It is a world where the church is a living organism, and my identity finds no completion apart from my relationship with my brothers and sisters in Christ. To be Abba's child, one must be willing to color outside the lines.

The Giving Tree

We feed over 10,000 people per week in our Bread of Life ministry that goes into over twenty churches and shelters. As a result, we are at the center of a group of churches of various denominations that the Lord is bringing together in unity. We have seen countless people in all different settings turn their lives over to Christ. Impromptu prayer services break out in pizza parlors, supermarkets, and in shelters. The church is everywhere. In addition, we are now involved in a plethora of agencies and organizations and bring the presence of Christ in there as well. Signs and wonders follow everywhere, and we have been blessed to see miracles from the very outset.

In our church, relationships take precedence over programs. We consciously make the economically unsound decision to invest our time and love in the human capital, which only God himself would choose to invest. We seek out the most broken and lead them into the world of grace. It is this world of grace that gives them significance, allowing them to lay their head on the beating heart of Jesus and radically redefine themselves as the "one whom Jesus loves." Living in the world of grace means living in a world of possibility where the word *impossible* does not exist and where we are all challenged to live courageously as children of God.

Faithful Bride

America is a vast mission field with countless opportunities to bring the message of the gospel of the kingdom. It is, however, what could be termed a "hidden mission field," where the hungry waste away alongside the rich, where the homeless sleep on the steps outside multi-million dollar church buildings, and countless souls perish having never heard the good news of Jesus Christ because their Christian neighbors never told them. America may arguably be one of the most difficult mission fields in the world because of a heart attitude characterized by apathy or being lukewarm. Our church without walls is located in Westchester County, just thirty minutes north of New York City. The reach of the church is Westchester County, north to Fairfield County, Connecticut, and south into the five boroughs of Manhattan. The "congregants" are of all races, nationalities, and ages, and church meetings take place on the streets, in homes, and in businesses. Westchester County itself, one of the wealthiest and most expensive areas in the United States, is riddled with contrasts and odd juxtapositions of ultra-rich neighborhoods abutting neighborhoods made up of the poorest of the poor.

While the vast majority of our ministry is to the poor and the homeless, it cuts across all economic, racial, social, and generational lines on any given day. No one-size-fits-all description would adequately encompass the people to whom we minister. In outward appearance, none are similar. Some arrive perfumed and coiffed, while others are covered in the stench of the wreckage of their human condition. Unbeknownst to them, however, there is a single common thread that unites them all, one common denominator—pain.

In the book of Ruth, her mother-in-law Naomi experiences circumstances that conspire to tell a story of a god who did not love her. Naomi never doubted God's existence. Her doubt was centered squarely on God's love for her. This is true for every modern-day Naomi as well. Broken relationships, broken homes, and financial struggles all continue to bear false witness to the fact that our pain does not truly matter to God. The deepest need of the broken and the poor is to know that God loves them and that he can and does meet them in their pain. Like Naomi, most do not doubt his existence. They doubt his goodness.

For these people, we are truly the hands and feet of Jesus. Our most important goal is to embrace them as we find them, love them unconditionally while continually reminding them that we are merely instruments to demonstrate the love of God. Love, in our view, is more than words. It is action. Love looks like something. To the hungry, love looks like food. To the homeless, love looks like a warm place to sleep. This is where their healing begins. Medical research has shown that deep relationships with others are just as important to humans as sleep or food.

The people to whom we minister are not only physically hungry, they are also hungry for a touch from God. All of their hope hinges not on a distant god, but on a loving Father who still cares enough to work miracles. Theology is of no use to the poor. They have need only for a gospel of power. Therefore, wherever we go and whatever our context, we always offer prayer. People line up for our food pantry and cry out before the distribution, "We want the blessing!" These are the unchurched asking for prayer. We have seen advanced cancer healed on numerous occasions. The paralyzed and the crippled have walked in the name of Jesus. Many have been delivered from drug or alcohol addictions and from mental illness. Perhaps the most startling work of the Holy Spirit has been the spontaneous and unsolicited confession of sins that often breaks out in rather public settings. Addicts repent of drug use, women repent of abortions, the married repent of extramarital affairs. Not only do the broken need to know God's love, they need to know his forgiveness. Love may be at the root of their healing, but grace is the key to their freedom. Therefore, a large component of our ministry consists of explaining and praying for God's grace and forgiveness. This way, the hungry leave not only full, but forgiven and free.

One modern-day Naomi came to our food pantry dirty and disheveled with a dazed look in her eyes. Her hair was greasy and multicolored after what appeared to be several failed attempts at a do-it-yourself coloring. Unable to stand still for more than a few seconds, she hopped from foot to foot in an odd, bird-like fashion. She spoke nonstop on every possible topic with little respect for any logical connection or sequence in the subject matter. Introduced to crack-cocaine as a teenager, she became a single mother at the age of sixteen. Her life derailed at that point, leading to a string of male abusers and a decades-long drug addiction, which had extended to at least one of her two sons. She was welcomed into our church just as she was. We showered her with love, acceptance, prayer, and helped to meet all of her physical needs.

One day, this Naomi arrived to help at the food pantry. Dressed in a brand new coat we had given her, the pleasant smell of perfume wafted up from her. Looking me straight in the eye, she announced, "I am beautiful because I am made in the image of God." Her lips, which were colored with bright red lipstick, curved into a broad smile to reveal one singular tooth. "Today is my birthday," she said happily, "and I believe God has a great plan for my life. I just might be the next Joyce Meyer." This is the sound of redemption!

The truth is every Naomi needs a Ruth. We have chosen to be the modern Ruth to the Naomis of our world. By loving the poor and the broken, their faith in the unconditional love of God is restored. This, in turn, gives them hope for the future. God's plan for redemption is always complete. God redeemed not only Naomi's life, but Ruth's life, the entire family line—and eventually the entire world through Jesus Christ. The ministry context for each and every one of us begins right under our own two feet. We are called to take dominion over the square foot of earth on which we are standing, to fight for our children, our spouses, our families, our neighborhoods, and for our country. We are all called to redeem the modern Naomis of our world, being assured that God's worldwide plan for redemption moves forward—one Naomi at a time.

2

The Faith Experience

What the World Needs

There is a classic children's book that seems to defy the traditional happy ending that accompanies virtually every children's story. It follows the lifelong relationship of boy and a tree, with the tree giving all it has to the boy as he grows. The story ends with the boy, now an old man, sitting down to rest on an old dry stump—all that is left of this once-magnificent tree. The last scene with the stump leaves the reader with a sense of hopelessness, wanting more. That is not the way stories are supposed to end, an inner voice protests. There must be hope for the tree.

There is hope, in fact, but it is found in a different book with a different ending.

> At least there is hope for the tree: If it is cut down, it will sprout again, and its new shoots will not fail. Its roots may grow old in the ground and its stump die in the soil, yet at the scent of water it will bud and put forth shoots like a plant. (Job 14:7-9)

Far from the world of either Job or a children's classic, is the modern media-saturated environment of twenty-first century America. News sources report with one voice the dismal state of world affairs. Cold war hostilities between the United States and Russia have reemerged with a vengeance. America and many other countries of the world, as I write this, are in turmoil in the wake of COVID-19. Previously unimaginable acts of terror are broadcasted while the whole world watches. Even weather patterns have inexplicably shifted, leaving one not knowing what to expect. The rules have changed without warning, and the media seems to give testimony only to fear and hopelessness. What is the answer? The answer is not a book. It's not even the Bible. The antidote to darkness is light. The answer for despair is hope. Religion can give no hope because it is form without substance. Hope is the good news of the new covenant. True hope can only come from the intimate relationship with God that is possible through Jesus Christ.

This type of intimacy gives rise to sounds of praise, regardless of circumstances. It bears witness to the goodness and the sufficiency of God. It attests to the fact that the one who has God, has all things. This is the sound of Psalm 23, which is arguably not only the most well-known psalm, but perhaps the most familiar passage in all of Scripture. In fact, it has become a type of secular icon, a symbol for both Christians and non-Christians alike. The challenge is to discover something new—a gem—in a familiar passage.

The most familiar extra-church setting for Psalm 23 is a funeral. Posing the question as to the reason behind its use at funerals is illuminative. It certainly isn't for the benefit of the deceased, who has no ears to hear the psalm's words. So we must conclude that it is for the benefit of the loved ones of the deceased. What precisely is it that benefits them in their time of grief? At its core, Psalm 23 is not about death; it is a poem, a song about life. It is a song about a life filled with hope amidst the darkest times because the psalm's author has chosen to put his trust in God. The message and the analysis are simple but far from simplistic. Psalm 23 is a message and a song whose notes resound louder, perhaps, in this day and age even than when it was written. If Psalm 23 is about the unshakable hope that comes from trust in God, then the twenty-first-century world needs a Psalm 23 experience.

The Faith Experience

Psalm 23 and the New Covenant

The contextual and historical distance between the modern-day reader and the original audience of the Psalms must be bridged in order to recover the full significance of Psalm 23. First and foremost is the fact that the Psalms were intended as songs. One view is that the book of Psalms was the hymn-book of the congregation of Israel during the existence of the Second Temple. If "faith comes from hearing the message, and the message is heard through the word about Christ" (Romans 10:17), then perhaps the Psalms are God's way of causing his people to believe.

Authorship of the psalm is attributed to David, and its probable inspiration was his personal experience of God's provision and faithfulness presented in familiar shepherding terms. David's life may be remote both historically and culturally to modern-day Western Christians, yet a common ground is found in his struggles, hardships, and pain. After being anointed as the king of Israel as a young boy, it would be approximately fifteen years before this prophetic act became a reality. In the meantime, David gained status and lost it, endured false accusations and slander, eventually to run away and hide in a cave with a band of disgruntled outcasts. Ultimately, in the midst of all these trials, David would have a revelation about God's character and of who he was in light of that revelation. He would learn to trust. Trust is at the very core of the intimacy that would eventually be his legacy as a "man after God's heart" (Acts 13:22).

In more general terms, the divine shepherding of the individual and the intimacy it entails give rise to some of the most beloved and touching passages in all of Scripture. God is depicted as a shepherd holding a rod over the sheep and noting each one as they pass under the rod to ensure that all are safely present (Ezekiel 34:16). God is also referred to as carrying lambs, guiding pregnant ewes (Isaiah 40:11), and seeking the lost and the weak (Ezekiel 34:16).

Ultimately, Jesus both teaches and displays the heart of the Father for each of the sheep. He is the Good Shepherd who calls each of the sheep by name, and his sheep know his voice (John 10:27). He leaves the rest of the flock to search after the one who has strayed and carries him home on his shoulders (Matthew 18:12). In an unexpected turn of events, something new is added. The Good Shepherd lays his life down for his sheep (John 10:11). The meaning of the metaphor cannot be missed. It portrays a relationship of complete trust and dependency by the sheep on the shepherd for their provision, care, and guidance. It is a deeply intimate relationship where each sheep is known, loved, and valued, and where each sheep knows the shepherd and will follow only him.

The needs of sheep help to define the qualities necessary to be a good shepherd. Shepherds are providers, protectors, and constant companions of the sheep. The shepherds have a close relationship with the sheep. This relationship is so close, in fact, that to this day, Middle Eastern shepherds are able to separate flocks that have mixed simply by calling the sheep by name. The sheep will follow only the voice of their shepherd. Both biblical writers and Jesus use the sheep/shepherd metaphor to construct a symbolic framework for certain key relationships.

Sheep are the most frequently mentioned animal in the Bible, with almost four hundred references if flocks are included. Shepherds are mentioned over one hundred times. Two factors contribute to their prevalence. The first is the prominent role sheep played in the agricultural life of the Hebrews. The second is the qualities of both shepherds and sheep and the nature of their interactions that make them excellent metaphors for spiritual realities. In the Middle East, sheep are not kept in pens but are moved from pasture to pasture during the day to prevent overgrazing. At night, the sheep are brought back into the sheepfold. The sheep's tendency to wander and their utter helplessness both to defend themselves against potential predators and to find their way make them totally dependent on the shepherd for food and water, protection, and guidance. The fact is, sheep cannot survive for long without a shepherd.

Psalm 23: A Psalm of David

> The Lord is my shepherd, I lack nothing.

The Faith Experience

> He makes me lie down in green pastures, he leads me beside quiet waters, he refreshes my soul. He guides me along the right paths for his name's sake.
>
> Even though I walk through the darkest valley, I will fear no evil, for you are with me; your rod and your staff, they comfort me.
>
> You prepare a table before me in the presence of my enemies. You anoint my head with oil; my cup overflows.
>
> Surely your goodness and love will follow me all the days of my life, and I will dwell in the house of the Lord forever. (Psalm 23:1-6)

Structurally, Psalm 23 is a sandwich that begins and ends with the use of the pronoun "he" in reference to the Lord, then rising to a crescendo of intimacy with the use of the pronoun "you" in the middle, verses four and five. Thematically, the psalm begins with a ringing declaration of the psalmist's relationship with the Lord and ends with the hope of returning home to his house.

The Lord is My Shepherd. I Lack Nothing

The Hebrew word translated as "Lord" in both verse one and verse six, the outer layers of the sandwich, is the word *Yahweh* or "I am who I am," the personal covenant name of God revealed to Moses on Mount Horeb (Exodus 3:14). David's use of God's covenant name evokes associations of Moses' meeting with God in the burning bush. That fateful meeting would mark the end of a forty-year exile for Moses and the beginning of a new relationship with the God of Israel, for both Moses and the entire nation.

> But Moses said to God, "Who am I that I should go to Pharaoh and bring the Israelites out of Egypt?" And God said, "I will be with you. And this will be the sign to you that it is I who have sent you: When you have brought

the people out of Egypt, you will worship God on this mountain." Moses said to God, "Suppose I go to the Israelites and say to them, 'The God of your fathers has sent me to you,' and they ask me, 'What is his name?' Then what shall I tell them?" God said to Moses, "I AM WHO I AM. This is what you are to say to the Israelites: 'I AM has sent me to you.'" (Exodus. 3:11-14)

The singular assurance given to Moses by the Lord of the mission's success was that he, Yahweh, would be with him. In other words, God's message to Moses was that he was enough. This very message is echoed in the words, "The Lord is my shepherd. I lack nothing."

The first verse of Psalm 23 proclaims to the hearer that God is enough. In other words, he who has Yahweh has everything he needs because he possesses the Giver of all good things. Moses had to understand this to come forth out of his exile and complete the impossible task set before him. David also understood this in his time of exile. Verse one is a simple declaration of what it means to have a relationship with the living God. In it can be heard the voices not only of Moses and David, but also of other Old Testament figures. In the opening chapters of the book of Ruth, the only characters are women. In a patriarchal society where women need men to be their protectors, providers, and voice, the reader is presented with three widows. To make matters worse, the two women of child-bearing age had been barren for a decade in a society that viewed barrenness as a curse from God.

The opening chapters of Ruth present an utterly hopeless situation. With no potential male redeemers in sight, the book of Ruth should be over before it begins. Astonishingly, however, the turning point comes when Ruth, a Moabitess, declares simply that God is enough.

> Where you go I will go, where you stay I will stay. Your people will be my people, and your God, my God. (Ruth 1:16)

The Faith Experience

Ruth, a foreigner, makes the life-altering choice to trust in a God she does not know, and that choice makes all the difference. This is the same choice set before the people by Moses:

> See, I set before you today life and prosperity, death and destruction. For I command you today to love the Lord your God, to walk in obedience to him, and to keep his commands, decrees and laws; then you will live and increase, and the Lord your God will bless you in the land you are entering to possess. (Deuteronomy 30:15-16)

Old Testament voices are not the only voices to be heard in Psalm 23. The sound of John's voice can also be heard here, as he leaned back on the heart of the living God, radically redefining himself as the "disciple whom Jesus loved."

> One of them, the disciple whom Jesus loved, was reclining next to him. Simon Peter motioned to this disciple and said, "Ask him which one he means." Leaning back against Jesus, he asked him, "Lord, who is it?" (John 13:23-25)

The religious spirit is always offering believers a substitute to keep us from having an intimate relationship with God, keeping us at a distance and offering works-based rituals instead of direct communion. In contrast, the voices of Psalm 23 are the voices of relationship, the voices of intimacy, the sound of Yahweh's children. They are the sound of the new covenant. The most often-cited reference to the new covenant in the Old Testament is:

> "The days are coming," declares the Lord, "when I will make a new covenant with the people of Israel and with the people of Judah. It will not be like the covenant I made with their ancestors when I took them by the hand to lead them out of Egypt, because they broke my covenant, though I was a husband to them," declares the Lord. "This is the covenant I will make with the people

of Israel after that time," declares the Lord. "I will put my law in their minds and write it on their hearts. I will be their God, and they will be my people. No longer will they teach their neighbor, or say to one another, 'Know the Lord,' because they will all know me, from the least of them to the greatest," declares the Lord. "For I will forgive their wickedness and will remember their sins no more." (Jeremiah 31:31-34)

The essence of the new covenant is the offer of relationship and intimacy, where each person has the opportunity to know God. The New Testament is in agreement, although it expresses the new covenant in slightly different terminology:

The Spirit you received does not make you slaves, so that you live in fear again; rather, the Spirit you received brought about your adoption to sonship. And by him we cry, "Abba, Father." (Romans 8:15)

Not only is intimacy with God the essence of the new covenant, but it is also the very definition of what it means "to know" God and is the core requirement of discipleship. In other words, the offer of a relationship must move from mere possibility into reality.

If you remain in me and my words remain in you, ask whatever you wish, and it will be done for you. This is to my Father's glory, that you bear much fruit, showing yourselves to be my disciples. (John 15:7-8)

Verse one of Psalm 23 contains a simple but profound message, one that is difficult to hear in a consumer-driven society: he who has God has all he needs. As a shepherd takes care of his sheep, so will God provide for the needs of his children. In the words of Jesus, "Seek first his kingdom and his righteousness, and all these things will be given to you as well" (Matthew 6:33). At this juncture, it is important to point out that this is not a prosperity doctrine. Just as a shepherd does not cater to every whim of the sheep, so does God not cater to every human desire. God is a caring shepherd, not Santa Claus. He provides for all the needs—not all of the wants—of those who choose to trust in him.

The disciples' instructions forced them to continually trust God for their provision.

> Calling the Twelve to him, Jesus began to send them out two by two and gave them authority over impure spirits. These were his instructions: "Take nothing for the journey except a staff—no bread, no bag, no money in your belts. Wear sandals but not an extra shirt. (Mark 6:7-9)

In fact, trusting in God's provision is one of the prerequisites for discipleship.

***

The Bread of Life Food Pantry

"I have no idea why you cannot understand that the Lord is your provider, not your ex-husband," bellowed the prayer minister into my face. She was losing patience with me as I made one last futile attempt to get her to understand the depth of my difficulties in caring for my children financially. At that time, I had no idea how to trust the Lord for finances. My ex-husband's first reaction on the day the gavel came down to mark our marriage's legal end was to cancel my health insurance and buy a beach pass for himself. Left with a mountain of debt, no health insurance, and no employment, the weight of the financial burden settled heavily upon my shoulders.

Thus I began my journey with God, sent out to declare the truth of the gospel with "no bread, no bag, nor any money in my belt." I had trusted God with my children, but could he be trusted with my mortgage?

"Put a food pantry in your home," I heard the Holy Spirit say to me in prayer one day.

"What? Here at our house?" I questioned what I had heard. "No one does that. No one puts a food pantry in an affluent neighborhood. Food pantries are located elsewhere," I pointed out to the Holy Spirit. Feeling a bit convicted, I continued to elaborate, "Food pantries are always in poorer neighborhoods where they are needed."

It was this very conviction, however, which caused me to obey what I had heard, and we began building a food pantry in our basement. Thus the Bread of Life food pantry was born, and I started learning what it means to trust in the Lord's provision. Within a few days, we awoke one morning to find cardboard boxes on our lawn. Thinking that someone had deposited his or her garbage in our yard while we slept, I was irritated. Immediately, I sent my boys out to clean up the mess. They returned in short order and announced, "Mom, it's not garbage. The boxes are filled with food!"

Within a few short months we had such an excess of donated food from area restaurants and grocery stores that we were forced to connect with an increasing number of local shelters, soup kitchens, and food pantries just to distribute it. We now feed thousands every week. For over a decade now, the Lord has provided faithfully for all of our needs, both personally and for the ministry. The rest, as they say, is history.

***

He Makes Me Lie Down in Green Pastures, He Leads Me Beside Quiet Waters, He Refreshes My Soul. He Guides Me along the Right Paths for His Name's Sake

To arrive at the most probable meaning of these beloved verses, they must be interpreted against the backdrop of Middle Eastern shepherding. Middle Eastern shepherds had to care for their sheep in a land comprised of dry rolling hills covered with sparse grass and where water sources were few and often seasonal. Given the historical context and contrary to the common understanding, it is reasonable to conclude that the intent behind the imagery in verses two and three is not primarily to evoke a sense of peace and rest. Instead, the focus is on life itself and on the shepherd as providing life to the sheep.

Such an interpretation ties in more seamlessly concerning restoring the "soul." The Hebrew word *nefesh*, often translated as "soul," also means

The Faith Experience

"life." The common understanding of *soul* among Western Christians as consisting of mind, will, and emotions has its origins in Platonic teaching introduced into Christian doctrine in the fifth century by Augustine. By way of contrast, the Hebrew understanding of *soul* is much more expansive and includes the very gift of life. Therefore, a more accurate rendering would be "he restores my life." Jesus is the fulfillment of the life-giving shepherd, and he says so explicitly, "I have come that they may have life and have it to the full. I am the good shepherd. The good shepherd lays his life down for the sheep" (John 10:10-11).

Psalm 23 presents a picture of abundant life in three statements, each speaking of the shepherd's influence over the flock. The shepherd makes the sheep lie down, makes them approach quiet waters so they can drink, and, in verse three, leads them faithfully on the correct paths. The two Hebrew verbs translated as "leads" both connote a gentle leading, not a forceful driving.

God leads the sheep along the "paths of righteousness" or right paths. Simply put, these are paths that will take a person to his or her ultimate destination. The shepherd leads the sheep along these right paths "for his name's sake." In the Hebrew culture, a personal name was believed to reveal the character of the individual, as well as their reputation (see Job 30:8). Thus, God leads the psalmist (and all of his people) along the right paths because this is his nature. God's actions as Shepherd are intentional and reveal his nature to human beings. The provision, protection, guidance, and unfailing love, which the shepherd provides for the sheep, together comprise a vivid metaphor for the security and abundance given to each person who chooses to walk in a relationship with God.

Even Though I walk Through the Darkest Valley, I Will Fear No Evil for You are with Me; Your Rod and Your Staff; They Comfort Me

As mentioned previously, Psalm 23 has been secularized and is thus familiar to both Christians and non-Christians alike. In particular, one is loathe to challenge the well-known and oft-recited version of verse four in the King James translation of *"Though I walk through the valley of the shadow of death, I will fear no evil."* Interestingly, however, there is no mention of the word *valley* anywhere in the Hebrew. The original Hebrew behind the "valley of the shadow of death" is *tsalmaveth*, a combination of two words, *tsel* (shadow) and *maveth* (death). When combined, there is the picture of "death-shadow" or a very deep darkness.

Also of interest is the Hebrew word *ra*, typically translated as "evil."[3] Psalms were often sung and not intended to be read silently, as the practice is today. Hence, *sound* is extremely important. The similarity in sound between the Hebrew word *ra* and the Hebrew word for shepherd, *ra`ah*[4] pits these two words directly against one another. While typically translated as "evil," *ra* has no simple English translation. It is the opposite of *shalom*, which is itself often inadequately translated as "peace." *Shalom* comes from the verb *shalem*, meaning "to complete." Therefore, *shalom* connotes completeness or wholeness in every respect, and encompasses the thoughts of justice, sufficient food, clothing, housing, divine health, and tranquility. *Ra*, as the absence of shalom, is chaos, disorder, and an utter lack of everything good. If shalom is wholeness or well-being, then *ra* is hopelessness. The Hebrew sound patterns put the shepherd, *ra`ah*, in direct opposition to hopelessness, *ra*.

ra'ah	*ra*
Shepherd	Chaos, disorder, lack of everything good

The rod and staff are those of a shepherd. In the Middle East, the shepherd carries a rod which is thrown at potential predators and is for protection. The shepherd's staff is used for guiding and counting the sheep. Together they symbolize the protection and care of the shepherd for the sheep.

---

3. "H7451 - ra` - Strong's Hebrew Lexicon (KJV)." *Blue Letter Bible*. Accessed 28 Jan, 2021. https://www.blueletterbible.org//lang/lexicon/lexicon.cfm?Strongs=H7451&t=KJV

4. "H7462 - ra`ah - Strong's Hebrew Lexicon (KJV)." *Blue Letter Bible*. Accessed 28 Jan, 2021. https://www.blueletterbible.org//lang/lexicon/lexicon.cfm?Strongs=H7462&t=KJV

In the midst of the darkest of shadows, the sheep has no fear for God is present with him or her. This affirmation that God's presence is enough to ensure safety is encapsulated in the phrase *"you are with me"* and is highlighted in the emphatic shift from the impersonal "he" to the more intimate "you." The assurance of God's presence begins and ends this psalm, as God's covenant name, *Yahweh*, is used only in verses one and six. God's presence, therefore, is all-surrounding.

You Prepare a Table Before Me in the Presence of My Enemies. You Anoint My Head With Oil; My Cup Overflows

In verse five, the metaphor has shifted from God as Shepherd to God as Host. To accept a person as a guest at one's table was not a meaningless gesture. To invite someone to dine at one's house was to set aside enmity and assume responsibility for that guest's safety while he or she was in the dwelling. To sit at Yahweh's table was to be in communion with him. This is done in full view of the guest's adversaries. In other words, the special relationship the child of Yahweh enjoys is declared publicly in a context of abundant blessing and security. This calls to mind God's provision for Israel during the Exodus when he fed them with manna from heaven.

> They willfully put God to the test by demanding the food they craved. They spoke against God; they said, "Can God really spread a table in the wilderness? True, he struck the rock, and water gushed out, streams flowed abundantly, but can he also give us bread? Can he supply meat for his people?" When the Lord heard them, he was furious; his fire broke out against Jacob, and his wrath rose against Israel, for they did not believe in God or trust in his deliverance. Yet he gave a command to the skies above and opened the doors of the heavens; he rained down manna for the people to eat, he gave them the grain

> of heaven. Human beings ate the bread of angels; he sent them all the food they could eat. (Psalm 78:18-25)

On a deeper level, though, verse five is the language of communion with God. It is the language of the new covenant.

> It is written in the Prophets: "They will all be taught by God." Everyone who has heard the Father and learned from him comes to me. No one has seen the Father except the one who is from God; only he has seen the Father. Very truly I tell you, the one who believes has eternal life. I am the bread of life. Your ancestors ate the manna in the wilderness, yet they died. But here is the bread that comes down from heaven, which anyone may eat and not die. I am the living bread that came down from heaven. Whoever eats this bread will live forever. This bread is my flesh, which I will give for the life of the world. (John 6:45-51)

Surely Your Goodness and Love Will Follow Me All the Days of My Life, And I Will Dwell in the House of the Lord Forever

Although the time during which David wrote the psalm is uncertain, one view is that Psalm 23 was written during the time of rebellion under Absalom. The basis for this view consists of the commonalities between Psalm 23 and other psalms written during this period; for example, Psalms 4 and 27. All of these psalms reflect David's longing to return home and to the house of God from the plains of Judah where he had retreated with his followers.

To be "in the house of the Lord," both literally and metaphorically, adds a communal dimension to this psalm, which for the first five verses most likely portrays the journey of the individual. In Psalms 23-30, the desire to dwell with God in his house is related to the theme of the

The Faith Experience

Exodus. The Jewish community in exile longed to return home to the second temple in Jerusalem, the spiritual center and unifying symbol of their faith. The communal theme is reinforced particularly when Psalm 23 is heard in conjunction with Psalm 22. The depth of trust portrayed in Psalm 23 is more fully appreciated in light of Psalm 22. Moreover, the ending of Psalm 22, with the psalmist in the congregation (Psalm 22:22, 25) would have been found in the house of the Lord (Psalm 23:6).

It is difficult for a society founded on individualism to hear, but the value of community is emphasized throughout the entire Bible. Yahweh's assurance to Moses was that the Hebrews would be delivered and would worship together on a mountain. The mountain called "Horeb," meaning "desolation," would then come to be known as the "mountain of God." In a similar vein, the book of Ruth closes with Ruth, once a foreigner and outsider, being embraced by the community who wishes upon her the blessings of Rachel and Leah, who together built up the house of Israel (Ruth 4:11).

The Hebrew word translated as "love" in the New International Version is *hesed*. *Hesed* is a difficult word to translate, as there is no exact English equivalent, but "unfailing love" might be a better translation. The Hebrew word *hesed* or "unfailing love" that is used in verse six, lies at the very heart of God's character. This word occurs twice in God's revelation of his character to Moses (Exodus 34:6-7). The Hebrew word *tov*, or "goodness," which appears in verse six of Psalm 23, is the same word used when God's "goodness" passed before Moses (Exodus 33:19).

While the majority of translators suggest that God's goodness and love will follow the psalmist, the Hebrew word *radaph* is actually very active in the sense of "to pursue; chase." In other words, God is in active pursuit of the psalmist.[5] The grammatical structure of the next Hebrew phrase being plural suggests continuance and can be more accurately

---

5. "H7291 - radaph - Strong's Hebrew Lexicon (KJV)." Blue Letter Bible. Accessed 28 Jan, 2021. https://www.blueletterbible.org//lang/lexicon/lexicon.cfm?Strongs=H7291&t=KJV

rendered as "days; lifetime" (all of my days).[6] Surely, goodness and unfailing love will pursue me all the days of my life, and I shall return, and having returned, dwell in the house of the Lord (Yahweh) all of my days. Is this not the very picture of the Father's love in Jesus' parable about the prodigal son?

> But while he was still a long way off, his father saw him and was filled with compassion for him; he ran to his son, threw his arms around him and kissed him. (Luke 15:20)

---

6. "H3117 - yowm - Strong's Hebrew Lexicon (KJV)." Blue Letter Bible. Accessed 28 Jan, 2021. https://www.blueletterbible.org//lang/lexicon/lexicon.cfm?Strongs=H3117&t=KJV

3

Encountering Christ

Psalm 23 and the Samaritan Woman

In Psalm 23, a chorus of voices throughout the ages can be heard. These voices give witness to what it means to live as a child of *Yahweh*, the God who gives hope to the hopeless and "gives life to the dead and calls things into being that were not" (Romans 4:17). Psalm 23 is the sound of a life redeemed, and eventually, a world redeemed. The Samaritan woman at the well may be nameless, but her story is timeless, and hers is one of the voices that can be heard in the notes of Psalm 23.

The story of the Samaritan woman at the well is told in the gospel of John. Unlike the other three synoptic gospels, the gospel of John is not primarily a chronological recounting of the life of Christ. Instead, its stated purpose is evangelistic in nature:

> Jesus performed many other signs in the presence of his disciples, which are not recorded in this book. But these are written that you may believe that Jesus is the Messiah, the Son of God, and that by believing you may have life in his name. (John 20:30-31)

The theology of John's gospel is delivered through the medium of contrasting metaphors, and the message of the unnamed Samaritan woman is no exception. It is strategically placed immediately following the account of Nicodemus. Examined side by side, these two juxtapose darkness with light, religion with faith, the respected with the nameless, the Jew with the Samaritan, and man with woman.

Betrayal, doubt, and deceit all take place under the cover of darkness. At night Judas leaves the upper room. Jesus is betrayed at night. Jesus is questioned at night and denied by Peter at night. The religious leader, Nicodemus grapples with Jesus' startling assertion of the need for a second birth at night. The opening of the story of the Samaritan woman stands in stark contrast to all of these. In her story, nothing is hidden. This meeting at the well takes place under the bright noonday sun in full view of all who care to see.

The Lord is My Shepherd. I Lack Nothing

> Now he had to go through Samaria. So he came to a town in Samaria called Sychar, near the plot of ground Jacob had given to his son Joseph. Jacob's well was there, and Jesus, tired as he was from the journey, sat down by the well. It was about noon. (John 4:4-6)

The text reads that Jesus "had," *edei*, to go through Samaria. Typically, pious Jews traveled around Samaria to avoid ritual defilement. Samaritans were considered unclean, occupying an odd intermediate position between Gentiles and Jews. The necessity of traveling through Samaria indicated by the use of the Greek word "had" (*edei*) is puzzling at first glance. Scripture underscores the fact that Jesus never moved in response to human pressure. In fact, when Lazarus lay ill and dying, Jesus steadfastly refused to respond to human pressure to go immediately to him, choosing instead to remain where he was for two more days (John 11:6). The movements of Jesus during his earthly ministry were directed solely by the Father's will. Therefore, the meeting at the well was not a chance meeting but one that was divinely ordained.

Encountering Christ

Jesus had a plan that was orchestrated by heaven. He "had" to go through Samaria to bring the Samaritan woman home.

> Suppose one of you has a hundred sheep and loses one of them. Doesn't he leave the ninety-nine in the open country and go after the lost sheep until he finds it? And when he finds it, he joyfully puts it on his shoulders and goes home. (Luke 15:4-6)

In Western society, inordinate value is placed on size and quantity. It seems that everything is supersized. There are mega-meals, mega-deals, and mega-churches. Jesus, on the other hand, continually demonstrated his heart to pursue the one lost sheep. He demonstrated that God's worldwide plan of redemption moves forward one person at a time. This was heard on the lips of the community at the close of the story when, in response to the witness of the woman, the whole community declared Jesus to be the "Savior of the world" (John 4:42).

Even Though I Walk Through the Darkest Valley, I Will Fear No Evil, For You Are with Me; Your Rod and Your Staff, They Comfort Me

> When a Samaritan woman came to draw water, Jesus said to her, "Will you give me a drink?" (His disciples had gone into the town to buy food.)
>
> The Samaritan woman said to him, "You are a Jew and I am a Samaritan woman. How can you ask me for a drink?" (For Jews do not associate with Samaritans.) (John 4:7-9)

From a cultural standpoint, virtually every detail in this story violates the social order. In fact, this conversation between Jesus and the Samaritan woman should never have taken place in the cultural reality of that time. As the story unfolds, however, it becomes increasingly clear that everything in the Samaritan woman's life is out of order. As Jesus, the Good Shepherd (*Ra'ah*) sits down by the well, he deliberately places himself in a position to deliver her from *ra*: "evil, disorder, and hopelessness." Interestingly, the way Jesus brings her life back into order, is by violating much of the social order.

In contrast to Nicodemus (a highly respected man of rank in the religious community), the Samaritan woman had no name. The absence of her name is pregnant with meaning. In Middle Eastern culture, someone's name was closely tied with their character and reputation. It symbolized the very essence of a person. To have a name was to have a good reputation. A bad reputation, conversely, meant one had no name at all.

Not only is this woman nameless, she is alone. It was customary for women to come together in groups to draw water as the water jars were heavy and difficult to lift. Moreover, the women usually came to draw water in the morning or in the evening hours to avoid the intense heat. The nameless Samaritan woman comes alone to draw water in the intense heat of the midday sun. The fact that she is alone under the scorching sun implies she is a social outcast, rejected by her community.

Middle Eastern customs included social taboos against a man speaking with an unaccompanied woman, particularly when there were no witnesses present. Propriety dictated that Jesus distance himself to allow this lone woman to approach the well. Instead, he remains seated directly in her path. Even more shocking to Middle Eastern sensibilities was Jesus' request. Jesus asked her for a drink of water. The Jews considered Samaritans to be unclean, as was anything they touched. Her bucket, therefore, is unclean. Jesus, a pious Jew, is undeterred by either the potential defilement from her bucket or the five-hundred-year-old hostility between the Jews and the Samaritans.

Jesus' paradigm for discipleship is upside down in relationship to the world. The fact that it is upside down means it is also costly. It requires humility, self-emptying, and sacrifice. It upends and roots out every presupposition and predisposition. Jesus' model of discipleship requires that the shepherd lay his life down for the sheep. Pride must be laid down at the feet of people who have none. Valuable time must be "wasted" on those society has deemed worthless. Jesus willingly, purposefully, and intentionally placed himself in a position of need with respect to the people whom he came to save—and he required no less of his disciples. They were to take nothing for the journey except a staff. No money, no bag, no bread, no extra clothing (Mark 6:8-9).

Jesus needed Peter's boat for a pulpit. Here, Jesus is thirsty and needs water, so he asks this Samaritan woman for a drink from her bucket. Humility has a see-saw effect. When the shepherd lays himself down, by definition, the sheep are raised up. This is the lesson of Jesus. By deliberately placing himself in need of what she has to offer, Jesus elevates her self-worth. Jesus changes the rules, turning the tables in a positive way. The woman's reaction is telling. Her response is literally, "Why are you, a Jewish male, talking to me, a woman—a Samaritan woman?" This literal translation shows her initial focus is on gender.

A complete understanding of the story of the Samaritan woman must address the issue of women, a topic dealt with in a cursory manner by most scholars in the context of this story. This is, after all, a story about Jesus and a woman. Her reaction underscores the importance of this violation of social norms. During his ministry, Jesus brought order and wholeness not only to her life, but also to the lives of all women with her. Jesus not only talked to women, but he invited them into his inner group of disciples and was financed by some of them (Luke 8:1-3).

When Michelangelo painted the ceiling of the Sistine Chapel in Rome, he painted two frescos of Eve. Next to the centerpiece is the fresco depicting Adam and Eve's expulsion from the garden of Eden. The center of the ceiling, however—and its focal point—features the creation of Eve. It has been noted that Michelangelo's paintings were greatly influenced by his theology. In his eyes, the creation of Eve is key for comprehending God's plan lost through the fall in the garden, and the ultimate restoration for which Jesus came and died.

Eve, the Samaritan woman, and every woman with her is designed together with Adam to be God's image-bearer (Genesis 1:27). The Samaritan woman, therefore, is part of this legacy Jesus came to restore. By blatantly ignoring the gender issue, by pressing in rather than retreating, and by deliberately placing himself in a position of need with respect to what she has to offer, Jesus at every turn affirms her as worthy of the respect due to her as a woman and divine image-bearer.

Eve, the Samaritan woman, and every woman with her were to carry out together with Adam—what theologians call the "cultural mandate." This was God's command to be fruitful and multiply, rule, and subdue the earth, which went beyond the physical, but was also spiritual and theological. The command "to be fruitful and multiply" applied to multiplying devoted worshipers of God and extending his rule and reign over the earth. During the course of his conversation with the Samaritan woman, Jesus once again breaks the rules and entrusts to this Samaritan woman what is arguably the deepest theological teaching about worship in the entire New Testament. It's not a coincidence that the teaching concerns God's desire for people who will worship him in spirit and truth. This is connected to her role in the cultural mandate, a role which she carries out by becoming a witness to her entire community.

He Makes Me Lie down in Green Pastures, He Leads Me Beside Quiet Waters, He Refreshes My Soul

> Jesus answered her, "If you knew the gift of God and who it is that asks you for a drink, you would have asked him and he would have given you living water."
>
> "Sir," the woman said, "you have nothing to draw with and the well is deep. Where can you get this living water? Are you greater than our father Jacob, who gave us the well and drank from it himself, as did also his sons and his livestock?"

Jesus answered, "Everyone who drinks this water will be thirsty again, but whoever drinks the water I give them will never thirst. Indeed, the water I give them will become in them a spring of water welling up to eternal life."

The woman said to him, "Sir, give me this water so that I won't get thirsty and have to keep coming here to draw water."

He told her, "Go, call your husband and come back."

"I have no husband," she replied.

Jesus said to her, "You are right when you say you have no husband. The fact is, you have had five husbands, and the man you now have is not your husband. What you have just said is quite true." (John 4:10-18)

This entire passage in the conversation between Jesus and the Samaritan woman is about life. It is also the place where religion and faith collide. The conversation Jesus had with the Samaritan woman in Sychar likely took place in full view of Mount Gerizim, the religious symbol of the Samaritan faith. The Samaritans themselves originated from the intermarriage between the Gentiles and the Israelites who were left behind during the Assyrian exile of the Northern Kingdom (2 Kings 17:24). They occupied a curious middle position between the Gentiles and the Jews and were considered a sect because of their veneration of Mount Gerizim as the Holy Mountain. The reference to Jacob's well and the later reference to Mount Gerizim (John 4:20) place this encounter within the framework of holy sites, which Jesus is shown to transcend. Holy sites were of great importance to both Jews and Samaritans. Thus, in full view of Mount Gerizim, Jesus—the one who would render it obsolete together with all other holy sites—is tired and sits down by the well.

The Jews considered the "gift of God" to be the Law and the Prophets. The Samaritans, however, restricted their canon to the Torah or the first five books of the Bible. Both groups were in agreement that the "gift of

God" was a book. However, the new covenant offered through Jesus consists not of a book, but a relationship with God through faith in Jesus. The "gift of God," in other words, is a person. It is Jesus Christ. "I will give you as a covenant for the people, a light for the nations" (Isaiah 42:6 ESV).

The woman's reference to Jacob's well is noteworthy as it has no basis in Torah or anywhere else in the Old Testament. Genesis does not contain any references whatsoever to Jacob ever owning a well, much less drinking of it and giving it to anyone else. In other words, this is sheer tradition. The term "living water" refers to spring water, which would have been a blessing of great value in the hot, dry climate of Palestine. Metaphorically, God was the spring of living water Judah had forsaken when they refused to trust God (Jeremiah 17:13). Jesus here uses the term "living water" to refer to himself.

The woman has religion along with the Torah and all of the accompanying traditions. Clearly, this religion is powerless to save, as her life is in complete disarray. Jesus does not dispute the validity of her traditions but simply offers to give her the living water that will bring her back to life. The living water is flowing over her, and she seems eager to receive it, but for all of the wrong reasons. She's not yet ready for the change that the living water can bring to her life. Her interest in the water is out of convenience. This water would mean the end of trips to fetch water, saving her time and energy. The woman wants religion, not a faith relationship. Religion is consumer-oriented. It is about receiving a product that will evoke positive emotions, provide a social community, and ease one's conscience. Religion never upsets the status quo because, ultimately, it is about being comfortable with it. Religion is form without substance and cannot provide the restoration this woman needs.

Faith, on the other hand, calls for risk. It hopes for destiny and can redeem all things. Faith gives life because it flows from a relationship with the source of all life—Jesus. The woman initially has no interest in becoming a spring of living water for others, maybe because it's not within the realm of the possible, given her history. Jesus, who gave Simon the new name "Peter" (the "Rock") because he knew who he would become, now casts a vision for her destiny as one of the greatest female evangelists in the Bible by asking her to be a witness to a man.

Jesus commands the Samaritan woman to go to her husband, convince him to come, and bring him back. By calling her to do this, Jesus once again is violating the social order. In the Middle East, women were not considered credible witnesses. Their testimony was not accepted in court, and they needed a male voice to testify on their behalf. Granted, this is not a courtroom setting, but in choosing to send a woman as a witness to a man, Jesus not only chooses to send a witness who possesses the "wrong" gender but who also has the "wrong" reputation. In John's gospel, the next time he makes such a request is when he instructs Mary Magdalene to go and witness to his brothers about his resurrection (John 20:17).

Contained within the command to go and be a witness are the seeds for the Samaritan woman's healing. Rabbinic law allowed only three marriages in a lifetime, even in the case of the death of previous husbands.[7] Presumably, the Samaritans maintained a similar limit. This woman, therefore, had more failed marriages than was even legally allowed. However, it is not (as most commentators conclude) irrefutable evidence that she was a serial fornicator or adulteress. A few decades before the birth of Jesus, a new type of divorce had been invented by Rabbi Hillel. It was called the "Any Cause" divorce and was a groundless divorce which could be initiated only by men. It did not require the man to prove his wife had done anything wrong and left her without any recourse. In fact, by the time Jesus was preaching in AD 30, groundless divorces had gained popularity, replacing divorces based on Old Testament grounds. By the time of Jesus, virtually every divorce was an "Any Cause" divorce, but the rabbis were still arguing about it. Their continued disagreement was reflected in the questions posed to Jesus (Matthew 19:3).

---

7. Taken from *Zondervan Illustrated Bible Backgrounds Commentary* by Clinton E. Arnold, General editor, copyright © 2002 by Zondervan. Used by permission of Zondervan.

The Giving Tree

Therefore, contrary to what some scholars have argued, there is no irrefutable evidence that this woman's life consisted of a series of sinful choices. If the former husbands had divorced her without reason using the "Any Cause" divorce prevalent among the Jews, what this woman had experienced was a lifetime of rejection by no fault of her own. But the text does make clear the present state of the woman's life: the woman is presently in an immoral relationship. If she is currently with an unmarried man, then questions arise as to why he does not marry her. If she is in an adulterous relationship with a married man, then the penalty for adultery under Mosaic Law is death, not divorce. In any case, Jesus exposes the true state of her life and the consequent need for the change, which will ultimately lead to her destiny.

He Guides Me Along the Right Paths for His Name's Sake

"Sir," the woman said, "I can see that you are a prophet. Our ancestors worshiped on this mountain, but you Jews claim that the place where we must worship is in Jerusalem."

"Woman," Jesus replied, "believe me, a time is coming when you will worship the Father neither on this mountain nor in Jerusalem. You Samaritans worship what you do not know; we worship what we do know, for salvation is from the Jews. Yet a time is coming and has now come when the true worshipers will worship the Father in the Spirit and in truth, for they are the kind of worshipers the Father seeks. God is spirit, and his worshipers must worship in the Spirit and in truth."

The woman said, "I know that Messiah" (called Christ) "is coming. When he comes, he will explain everything to us."

Encountering Christ

Then Jesus declared, "I, the one speaking to you—I am he." (John 4:19-26)

The Samaritan woman's reaction to the unexpected revelation of her life's truth is an attempt to divert the unwanted attention to a theological discussion. The unexpected exposure has caused her to retreat into the safety of religion. Men did not typically engage in theological discussions with women; in fact, some rabbis held that excessive talk with any woman—even one's own wife—was a diversion of valuable time that could be used to study the Torah.[8] However, Jesus is on a mission: "That she may have life, and have it to the full" (John 10:10). Once again, he overturns the accepted state of affairs and acts toward her in a way that is anything but typical. Not only is he willing to discuss theology with this woman, but he also singles her out as the recipient of one of the most important New Testament teachings on worship. Once again, Jesus elevates her status as a person and that of all women with her.

Having gone down all the wrong paths in her life, Jesus now carefully leads the Samaritan woman down the path that will take her where she needs to go. Jesus tells her explicitly what he only implied in his conversation with Nicodemus. In doing this, Jesus nullifies one of the primary sources of contention between the Jews and Samaritans by declaring both Jerusalem and Mount Gerizim obsolete. True worship has nothing to do with a place; instead, it comes through a relationship with Jesus Christ. Only those born of the Spirit can worship in Spirit and in truth (John 3:5-8). The Father seeks those who worship in Spirit and in truth (John 4:23). He seeks those who are born from above (John 3:7). God wants to be their Father, and he wants their worship. Just as the Father is seeking these true worshipers, so is Jesus, the Good Shepherd, seeking "sheep not of this sheep pen" (John 10:16).

Having entrusted to her this groundbreaking revelation about worship, Jesus is far from finished. He concludes the astonishing discourse with the first of the list of "I AM" statements in John's gospel.

---

8. Taken from *Zondervan Illustrated Bible Backgrounds Commentary* by Clinton E. Arnold, General editor, copyright © 2002 by Zondervan. Used by permission of Zondervan.

Significantly, this is the only instance in which Jesus directly reveals his identity as the Messiah before he is questioned by the chief priests and teachers of the law (Luke 22:66-70). The other "I AM" statements contained in the gospel of John are couched in terms of metaphor. The phrase "I AM" that appears in the Greek text is the exact phrase used in the Greek Old Testament to translate "*Yahweh*," the original Hebrew of God's covenant name given to Moses from the burning bush. In an interesting parallel, Jesus speaks clearly to this woman, just as God spoke clearly to Moses. The Lord contrasted how he spoke to other prophets in dreams and visions with how he spoke to Moses, "With him I speak face to face, clearly and not in riddles; he sees the form of the Lord" (Numbers 12:8).

The Samaritan woman's story profoundly illustrates what it means to have an encounter with the living God. She begins the journey as a woman who has never quite measured up to the expectations of others or managed to live up to the requirements of her religion. The voice of religion surely says, "She's gotten exactly what she deserves." However, Jesus dispels all the notions of a distant and angry god, restoring her very life and leading her down the right paths, all for his name's sake. The Samaritan woman is a picture of one the Father seeks—worshipers who are born of the Spirit; children who walk in a Psalm 23 relationship with him.

You Prepare a Table Before Me in the Presence of My Enemies. You anoint My Head with Oil; My Cup Overflows

> Just then his disciples returned and were surprised to find him talking with a woman. But no one asked, "What do you want?" or "Why are you talking with her?"
>
> Then, leaving her water jar, the woman went back to the town and said to the people, "Come, see a man who told

me everything I ever did. Could this be the Messiah?" They came out of the town and made their way toward him.

Meanwhile his disciples urged him, "Rabbi, eat something."

But he said to them, "I have food to eat that you know nothing about."

Then his disciples said to each other, "Could someone have brought him food?"

"My food," said Jesus, "is to do the will of him who sent me and to finish his work. Don't you have a saying, 'It's still four months until harvest'? I tell you, open your eyes and look at the fields! They are ripe for harvest. Even now the one who reaps draws a wage and harvests a crop for eternal life, so that the sower and the reaper may be glad together. Thus the saying 'One sows and another reaps' is true. I sent you to reap what you have not worked for. Others have done the hard work, and you have reaped the benefits of their labor." (John 4:27-38)

The disciples arrive, and suddenly, the picture shifts. Upon their return from their trip, they are surprised to find Jesus alone and engaged in a theological discussion with a woman—a Samaritan woman. Once again, the tables have been turned. Once an outsider, the Samaritan woman is now the insider, while the disciples, once insiders, are now the observers. The outcast, the Samaritan, the woman is on the inside. The disciples, the Jews, the men are on the outside. This story's shift is similar to the shift in Psalm 23, when God becomes the host. The Samaritan woman has been invited to dine at Jesus' table, in communion with him. "Here I am! I stand at the door and knock. If anyone hears my voice and opens the door, I will come in and eat with that person, and they with me" (Revelation 3:20). Jesus is laying a table before her in the presence of her enemies. Soon the community which once rejected her will also witness her acceptance by the Messiah.

The Giving Tree

The Samaritan woman immediately withdraws and, leaving her water jar, goes back into the village on a mission. No detail is insignificant; neither is the fact that she leaves her water jar behind. First and foremost, such details give credence to the fact that this is an eyewitness account—a detail an eyewitness would remember. John's gospel is filled with such nuances, such as how the house was filled with the fragrance of perfume as Mary anointed the feet of Jesus (John 12:3). These details are given so that "you may believe that Jesus is the Messiah, the son of God, and that by believing you may have life in his name" (John 20:31). On a more symbolic level, the woman leaves her water jar the same way that the disciples left their nets (Mark 1:18; Matthew 4:20-22). The Samaritan woman not only fulfills the original command given her by Jesus to get her husband and bring him back, but also goes well beyond the original mandate and witnesses to the entire community. Not only does this woman receive the living water Jesus offered, but she becomes a spring for others.

There are two types of water and two types of food mentioned in the story. The Samaritan woman comes for (and Jesus asks for) physical water to quench a physical thirst. In return, Jesus offers her living water to quench her spiritual thirst. From the beginning of the story, the disciples focus on physical food. They return from town with food only to find that Jesus has food about which they know nothing. The disciples' thoughts are on Jesus' physical needs. In contrast, Jesus' focus is on his spiritual food—to complete the work of the Father. In fact, food was sometimes used as a metaphor in the Old Testament for one's calling (Jeremiah 15:16; Ezekiel 2, 3).

Jesus lived transparently in front of his disciples, modeling the concepts and values which he taught. In his model for discipleship, Jesus challenged his disciples at every turn to reevaluate their underlying suppositions and paradigms, to grow into their calling, and to value people above custom or expediency. The Father had a plan for this Samaritan woman's life. Therefore, Jesus "had" to go through Samaria to meet with her. The fruit of this meeting would be the "harvest" of the entire village, a harvest which would be completed in two days (John

4:40-43). Jesus had been sowing during the disciples' absence in the village. Plowing usually took place in September, and reaping would occur in the following April or May. The prophet Amos had a vision of hope and restoration, where the two actions would converge in time. Jesus appears to be claiming this for his own ministry.

> "The days are coming," declares the Lord, "when the reaper will be overtaken by the plowman and the planter by the one treading grapes. New wine will drip from the mountains and flow from all the hills, and I will bring my people Israel back from exile. They will rebuild the ruined cities and live in them. They will plant vineyards and drink their wine; they will make gardens and eat their fruit." (Amos 9:13-14)

Surely Goodness and Love Will Follow Me All the Days of My Life, and I Will Dwell in the House of the Lord Forever

Many of the Samaritans from that town believed in him because of the woman's testimony, "He told me everything I ever did." So when the Samaritans came to him, they urged him to stay with them, and he stayed two days. And because of his words many more became believers. They said to the woman, "We no longer believe just because of what you said; now we have heard for ourselves, and we know that this man really is the Savior of the world." (John 4:39-42)

In just two days, Jesus resurrects the Samaritan woman from the ranks of the walking dead, restores her life, and repositions her in a place of respect within her community. David's journey in Psalm 23 ends with his return to the "house of the Lord." The story of the Samaritan woman ends in the same place. During his discourse on worship, Jesus rendered both Mount Gerizim and Jerusalem obsolete. The "house of the Lord" was not a place at all. It was in the community of people who worship in Spirit and truth. The Good Shepherd "had" to go through Samaria to pursue a lost sheep and carry her home to his house, the newly transformed Samaritan community of worshipers.

The Samaritans initially believe based on the woman's testimony, which is then reinforced by the word of Jesus (John 4:41). The Samaritans were not looking forward to a messianic ruler, as were the Jews. Instead, they were anticipating a type of prophet who would speak what God commanded (see Deuteronomy 18:18). Their encounter with Jesus caused their expectations to expand greatly, looking beyond a teacher to a savior. The expression "Savior of the World" is used only twice by John, once in this gospel and in John's first epistle (1 John 4:14). This is an expression peculiar to John and reflects a viewpoint that God's love and redemptive plan for the world are displayed through Jesus (John 1:29; 3:16). Interestingly, this role of Jesus as Savior of the World is proclaimed by Samaritans and stands in stark contrast to the Pharisee's complaints as Jesus entered Jerusalem: "The whole world has gone after him" (John 12:19).

The Tree of Life

There is hope for every person who has given until he or she can give no more. There is hope for every victim of abuse and betrayal. There is hope for our troubled world. True hope is found in the trust in God that is the hallmark of faith. It comes through experience and intimacy with Jesus Christ. Such an experience is deeply personal, life-giving, and transformative, and it can be neither counterfeited nor mass-produced. To know God is to have a Psalm 23 experience. It transforms God from the distant and angry god of religion and redefines him as the Good Shepherd who loves enough to lay down his life for the sheep. It also brings order and wholeness to shipwrecked lives, radically renaming the Samaritan woman, and all people with her, "the one whom Jesus loves." Encounter, relationship, and experience are the essence of what it means to "know" God, which is at the heart of the new covenant.

Encountering Christ

Psalm 23 is the sound of hope. It is the song of the children of God throughout the ages. It is the song of Moses, David, Ruth, and the Samaritan woman. It is the song of the modern-day disciple who knows by experience that God is enough. As the Samaritan woman knows, religion can never satisfy. It has no power to transform or change lives. In fact, it resists an encounter at all costs—because an encounter demands vulnerability and entails exposure. Religion is passive and consumer-oriented. It is about products, not people. An experience, on the other hand, demands participation and partnership. Relationship is time-consuming, risky, and costly. It upends the status quo. This is the model of discipleship Jesus presented in his ministry.

Jesus offered a relationship, a journey, and a destiny to every sheep he "had" to rescue and every person he "had" to go out of his way to restore. He invited them all to his table, gave life to their broken lives, and released them to help him usher in his kingdom. There is hope for this world. There is good news. It is not a book, nor is it religion. It is Jesus himself. He is the "gift of God" who arose out of the stump of Jesse:

> A shoot will come up from the stump of Jesse; from his roots a Branch will bear fruit. The Spirit of the Lord will rest on him—the Spirit of wisdom and of understanding, the Spirit of counsel and of might, the Spirit of the knowledge and fear of the Lord—and he will delight in the fear of the Lord. He will not judge by what he sees with his eyes, or decide by what he hears with his ears; but with righteousness he will judge the needy, with justice he will give decisions for the poor of the earth. He will strike the earth with the rod of his mouth; with the breath of his lips he will slay the wicked. Righteousness will be his belt and faithfulness the sash around his waist.
>
> The wolf will live with the lamb, the leopard will lie down with the goat, the calf and the lion and the yearling together; and a little child will lead them.

The Giving Tree

The cow will feed with the bear, their young will lie down together, and the lion will eat straw like the ox. The infant will play near the cobra's den, and the young child will put its hand into the viper's nest. They will neither harm nor destroy on my holy mountain, for the earth will be filled with the knowledge of the Lord as the waters cover the sea. (Isaiah 11:1-9)

4

Transformed by Love

Mute Christianity

The true Christian witness has gone silent in twenty-first-century America. It is evident that the church's effect on the surrounding culture is insignificant and on the decline. Most Americans who consider themselves Christians have been lulled into a sense of complacency and would be shocked to find out that many consider America to be one of the largest mission fields in the world. Anti-Christian sentiment is increasingly prevalent in the United States. The separation of church and state originally intended to ensure the state was kept out of the church is now used to ensure the church is kept out of the state—and virtually everywhere else.

How has this state of affairs arisen? Where is the sound of the Christian witness in America, and why is it the church has not taken seriously the Great Commission to "go and make disciples of all nations" (Matt. 28:19), becoming instead a nation to be discipled? The answer is shockingly simple: American Christianity has substituted religion for relationship and complexity of programming for the simplicity of the gospel. Taught to be satisfied with little, nominal Christianity has become the norm, in effect forfeiting the abundant life Jesus promised for crumbs from the Father's table. Thus, the sound of the Christian witness has gone silent, and the church has become ineffectual, something to be influenced instead of a catalyst for change. The boundaries have shifted. The lines have been blurred. The American church has been fenced in. Will no childlike voice speak out against the conspiracy that the emperor is finely dressed and well-fed, when in fact, he is starving, bloated, and naked? Indeed, the emperor isn't wearing any clothes.

> To the angel of the church in Laodicea write: These are the words of the Amen, the faithful and true witness, the ruler of God's creation. I know your deeds, that you are neither cold nor hot. I wish you were either one or the other! So, because you are lukewarm—neither hot nor cold—I am about to spit you out of my mouth. You say, "I am rich; I have acquired wealth and do not need a thing." But you do not realize that you are wretched, pitiful, poor, blind and naked. I counsel you to buy from me gold refined in the fire, so you can become rich; and white clothes to wear, so you can cover your shameful nakedness; and salve to put on your eyes, so you can see. Those whom I love I rebuke and discipline. So be earnest and repent. Here I am! I stand at the door and knock. If anyone hears my voice and opens the door, I will come in and eat with that person, and they with me. (Revelation 3:13-20)

Recovering the Genius of John Wesley

If the church itself is ineffectual, then the Christian witness itself must have become ineffectual. Where, indeed, are all the disciples who were commissioned to be witnesses for Jesus Christ? Unfortunately, the church of the twenty-first century is not the first to face this question nor wrestle with this problem. The Christian witness might appropriately be called the question for the ages. Many voices throughout the history of Christianity had, at differing times, the audacity to proclaim the church wanting and the Christian witness elusive. One of these voices was that of John Wesley, the founder of Methodism.

Transformed by Love

John Wesley was a man for the people. His approach to Christianity, theology, and the gospel was elegantly simple. It was efficient, effective, transformative, communicative, and powerful. Paradoxically, though, the very complexity and academic disconnectedness against which he fought during his lifetime is what has obscured his true genius. The value of Wesley's contribution to the Christian heritage and Christian discipleship, in particular, has been dramatically undervalued due to his overwhelming success in actually fulfilling the Great Commission of Jesus. John Wesley burned with a passion for sharing the gospel of Jesus Christ and was committed to carrying it from one end of the country to the other. He believed the gospel had the power to transform lives, and by transforming lives, the nation could ultimately be transformed.

John Wesley was an evangelist, and it was this role that rendered him academically suspect. The fact that John Wesley was not a theologian's theologian with a theology worked out in academia's isolation is arguably the very factor behind his success. Instead, he was an evangelist with a theology worked out in real-life situations on the mission field. For Wesley, all questions of doctrine were secondary to sharing the gospel. He maintained a distinct distaste throughout his life for quarreling about words, which he viewed as a distraction from the primary goal of evangelism.

John Wesley never lost focus on the main mission: to raise up disciples for Jesus Christ; disciples whose lives were transformed and had the potential to transform others through their witness. John Wesley's Christianity was dynamic and alive. It was radical and powerful. It communed with, cooperated with, and supported others. It was forged in the fires of the mission field and in the context and reality of people's lives. Therefore, it was relevant, effective, and life-changing. John Wesley's Christianity was the story of what it meant to be a disciple of Jesus Christ. Christianity was a lifestyle, a continuum of decisions, not a single decision. Above all, John Wesley's Christianity was simple. John Wesley's genius rests precisely in this simplicity.

The Giving Tree

Theologians dispute the key contribution of John Wesley to Christian history. Some emphasize his distinctive doctrines of justification and sanctification. Others point to his method of discipleship, which consisted of small groups called "classes" or "bands." The significance of both of these is indisputable. Ultimately, however, they miss the mark because they miss the heart of the man himself. John Wesley had searched for God and found him. His goal was to share his experience with others on as broad of a scale as possible. He believed in a Christianity, in a gospel, in good news that was truly good news because it changed lives. He tested his theology and method by the fruit they bore; for example, he examined the transformation in the lives of the Methodists. The most logical approach to evaluating John Wesley, thus, is a Wesleyan one. To answer the question as to John Wesley's genius, one must inquire into which single factor contributed most to the transformation in John Wesley's life as well as the change in the lives of others.

Indisputably, Wesley's legacy to the succeeding generations was comprised of several key components, all of them threads woven into the tapestry of the whole of the Christian life. Arguably none of those elements was entirely original in any meaningful sense. However, Wesley was radical in his focus, in his passion, and most of all, in his simplicity. These were the factors that were evidenced as fruitfulness in his life. Any examination of John Wesley should never lose sight of the proverbial forest for the trees by substituting the component parts of his approach or his theology for his grand vision. John Wesley was an evangelist. The essence of his message was the gospel of Jesus Christ. He believed that the essence of the church's mission was evangelistic. His emphasis was, therefore, on living faith.

In Wesley's world, nominal Christianity did not exist. Simply put, for John Wesley, every Christian should be a disciple, and the hallmark of a disciple was a life transformed by and into love. For John Wesley, this was true Christianity, which had the potential to turn the world upside down. John Wesley invited people to enter into a simple paradigm of faith—a relationship with God, nothing added. The "God is enough" doctrine of John Wesley is the sound of the new covenant and the heart of New Testament faith. It pushes aside religion and offers something simple, real, and life-changing. Changed lives have the power to change lives. John Wesley remains relevant to twenty-first-century America because the gospel is still relevant to the church of twenty-first-century America.

A Simple Message: Love

John Wesley's message was the gospel in simple terms for all people. It was worked out in the context of the mission field and presented in a way accessible to all people, regardless of educational or social background. He believed that being a Christian was a lifelong journey and that every Christian's goal was to be a disciple of Jesus Christ. Christian lives should reflect the Christian faith. In other words, faith was manifested in the life of a believer as he or she was transformed in increasing measures into the likeness of Christ. The likeness of Christ, or "holiness," was the essence of the Christian witness.

According to John Wesley, the Christian disciple was forgiven, born again as a child of God, and then set on a lifelong journey of being formed into the image of Christ—being made holy.

The process of being made holy is called sanctification. Wesley was adamant that both justification and sanctification were the result of grace and through faith in God. Faith was the only condition for justification, and so it was for sanctification as well. Wesley was convinced that God's sanctifying grace extended throughout the Christian life and that this grace made possible entire sanctification—or Christian perfection—during this lifetime. It was a dynamic process, a polemic between God's grace and human free will.

Wesley's so-called "second blessing" was comprised basically of the process by which God so filled the believer's heart with love that the power of sin was broken and holiness the result. A work of grace subsequent to regeneration had not been emphasized since the fourth century. Although Wesley's emphasis was on the cleansing process instead of the power imparted by the "baptism of the Holy Spirit," his second blessing set the stage for the Pentecostal/Charismatic movement of the twentieth century. Remarkably, Pentecostal historian Vinson Synan has referred to John Wesley as the father of the modern Pentecostal movement.

According to Wesley, Christian perfection or holiness was to be every Christian's goal, thus the ultimate aim of discipleship. For Wesley, holiness was not optional but was instead fundamental for the Christian life. Since Wesley viewed evangelism as the church's primary mission, he was intentionally cognizant of the impact of the Christian witness, although he did not use that terminology. John Wesley was determined to reform not just the church but also the entire nation. Such a sweeping vision of reformation was contingent on the Christian witness's influence throughout the land, the witness of a life transformed. John Wesley had a grand but simple mission with a grand but simple message. That message was the possibility of achieving holiness during this lifetime. This was the essence of the Christian life and witness for Wesley.

Wesley made a strong statement about how important holiness is when he claimed that holiness is religion itself. The concept of holiness was a core belief of the Methodist movement. In his messages, Wesley's commonly showed the contrast between nominal and true Christianity, calling nominal believers "Almost Christians," and true believers "Altogether Christians."

Due largely to misunderstanding of what Wesley intended by "Christian perfection," holiness is arguably not only the most well-known, but also the most often disputed point of Wesley's doctrine. Simply put, Wesley's doctrine of Christian perfection has been largely misunderstood due to a failure to recognize that, for Wesley, Christian perfection did not imply sinlessness. Rather, Wesley defined Christian perfection or entire sanctification as the fulfillment of what Jesus termed were the two greatest commandments—love of God and love of neighbor.

> It is thus that we wait for our entire sanctification, for a full salvation from all sins, from pride, self-will, anger,

unbelief, or as the apostle expresses it, "Go on to perfection." But what is perfection? Here it means perfect love. It is love excluding sin; love filling the heart, taking up the soul's whole capacity.[9]

For Wesley, Christian perfection was the ultimate goal of the Christian life. That perfection was ultimately defined by an inward renewal of the human being to love the Lord with all of the mind, heart, soul, and strength and love neighbor as oneself. Thus, a mature disciple was one for whom consistent obedience had become so habitual as to crowd out intentional sin, but did not exclude the possibility of unintentional sin by mistake or ignorance. Wesley believed that a life marked by such an overwhelming love for God and neighbor was intended to be the norm for the Christian life rather than the exception. The doctrine of Christian perfection was not simply one of many doctrines for Wesley; it was the heart of Methodism. In other words, Methodism consisted of many structures, but the house itself was built of holiness. For Wesley, holiness was the goal of the Christian life.

Wesley's doctrine on Christian perfection brought him into conflict with the Calvinists. The Calvinists firmly believed that Christ had fulfilled the requirements of the law by proxy and that his righteousness was imputed to the believer by faith. Under the Calvinist position, the sinner clearly remained a sinner. Therefore, it would have been presumptuous for a sinner to aspire to any type of perfection other than that imputed to him by faith. Practically, Calvinist theology led to complacency on the part of Christians, the allowance for sin, and confusion as to the nature of the Christian life. Equivocating earning with effort, the Calvinists were interpreted as implying that human effort was precluded by grace.

Thus, in the mission field, Wesley encountered both confusion and complacency. At its extreme, Calvinism posed the threat of practical antinomianism—complete freedom from the moral law. The Calvinist view of justification with the imputed righteousness of Christ

---

9. Taken from *The Works of John Wesley, Vol 2*, "The Scripture Way of Salvation," by John Wesley. Copyright © 1984 by John Wesley. Used by Permission of Zondervan.

implied that there was nothing the believer could do in this lifetime toward self-improvement, so logically, the believer was relieved of any responsibility to keep the moral law. It may have been precisely this struggle against the potential for lawlessness and its diminishing effect on the Christian witness which served as the impetus for Wesley to reject the imputed form of righteousness as the fulfillment of the law by proxy. If Christ had fulfilled all the requirements of the law on behalf of the human race, this seemed to remove any obligation to fulfill the moral law altogether. [10]

Wesley believed that Christian perfection was real, not imputed. For Wesley, perfection should be palpable, visible, and meaningful, not an act of divine deception where God no longer saw the sin present in a believer's life. John Wesley formulated instead a doctrine of justification that allowed for God's grace and called for Christian accountability. In other words, for Wesley, grace was opposed to Christian earning, but not to Christian effort. Wesley disassociated the fulfillment of the law from justification and attached it instead to sanctification. According to Wesley, sanctification was quite distinct from justification, although it was also in response to faith and imparted by grace. For John Wesley, the logical conclusion of a life submitted to God's grace was that holiness evidenced by love was the norm for Christian life, and average Christianity was no Christianity at all. For Wesley, the everyday Christian life was intended to be extraordinary.

History bears witness to the legacy of "normal" Christians who have chosen to love and live in extraordinary ways. Some, such as Mother Teresa, have touched the world with their profound acts of love and charity. Others, unrecognized by the world, have touched their neighborhoods.

***

---

10. David Watson, *The Early Methodist Class Meeting: Its Origins and Significance* (Eugene, OR: Wipf & Stock Pub, 2002), 60.

Transformed by Love

Rachelle

I stood at the pulpit, silently praying that I would be able to make it through the eulogy for one of my dearest friends. Looking out into the audience, I saw people of every age, economic background, and nationality. The church was packed to overflowing with standing room only. They had all come to celebrate an extraordinary woman whose valiant battle with cancer had impacted them all. As I was preparing the words I would say to honor my friend, nothing seemed to suffice.

"Preach the gospel," I heard the Holy Spirit say.

"At a funeral, Lord?" I questioned.

As I gazed out at the crowd, I knew it was perfect, not only for the Holy Spirit, but it was also what Rachelle would have wanted. I recalled the first moment I saw her. She was in a hospital bed, very ill with cancer. As I began to worship the Lord and pray for her healing, I felt such a love for her that I knew at once the love was not my own. This was the love of the Father.

It was my fiftieth birthday, and I heard myself say, "Lord, if I could have anything for my birthday, I would like to see this woman healed." Rachelle was healed that day, completely healed. She recorded her testimony of the Lord's healing, and we uploaded it to the Internet for all to hear. Rachelle was cancer-free for approximately two years. Then one day, the news came—the cancer had returned. Over the next three years, it was somewhat of a rollercoaster ride, with Rachelle having extremely good periods interwoven with what could only be called near-death experiences. I watched the Lord raise Rachelle from her near deathbed no less than five times as we would be called in to pray while she was in a coma.

My husband came with me the last time I saw her. As we came in, Rachelle was unconscious, and I immediately sensed that something was different this time. I sensed it, but I didn't want to believe it. Five years had passed since I met Rachelle. I had come to believe that God had healed her countless times, and he would heal her this time too. Only this time, I heard nothing. The silence was deafening.

"Lord," I called out to the Holy Spirit, "what would you have me do here?" This time there was no answer. I heard nothing, so I prayed on my own, whatever I could think of—anything, pleading with God for healing.

At one point, she surprisingly woke up, looked at me, and said, "You look beautiful today," before she slipped back into unconsciousness.

As we walked out, my husband shook his head. Several days later, we received the news that Rachelle had gone home to be with Jesus. To say that Rachelle was extraordinary would be an understatement. I never heard her complain once through all of her sickness and pain. She was forever grateful, thankful, and always had faith in the goodness of God. She had a love for people that was transformative—it knew no color, judgment, or pride. We nicknamed her "God's little lamb" because of her gentleness of spirit and kindness toward all. Rachelle was a light, a life well-lived. She lived well because she had loved well, both God and neighbor.

***

A Simple Method: Community

John Wesley's broad influence stemmed from not only the simplicity of his message, but also of his method. To him, the two were inseparable. Wesley's experience on the mission field had convinced him that holiness couldn't be achieved in isolation. He had observed firsthand on the mission field the struggles of Christians trying to work out their salvation by themselves. Moreover, John Wesley pointed out the lack of any biblical basis for Christian isolationism. Neither Jesus nor the apostles ever commanded anyone to withdraw from the world into solitude; on the contrary, Jesus modeled withdrawal only during times of prayer with the Father. Jesus spent the majority of his time engaging with people as an active participant in everyday life and the world.

John Wesley was a vocal opponent of so-called Christian practices that isolated Christians from one another. He believed that it was impossible to grow in the love of God and neighbor in isolation. Consequently, he held very strong opinions in opposition to the spirituality of the Mystics and made bold statements to that effect. In his preface to the 1739 edition of Hymns and Sacred Poems, he wrote:

> Directly opposite to this (referring to the Mystics) is the gospel of Christ. Solitary religion is not to be found there. "Holy Solitaries" is a phrase no more consistent with the gospel then "holy adulterers." The gospel of Christ knows of no religion but social and no holiness but social holiness.[11]

This statement by Wesley argued the importance of community for growth in holiness and excluded the possibility of Christian holiness in isolation. The inherent logic in Wesley's assertion leaves little room for dispute. If holiness is defined by love, how exactly does one learn to love one's neighbor in isolation? Love is not static. It is an action, a verb that requires an object.

John Wesley's insistence on the necessity of social holiness continued throughout his life. On August 25, 1763, with two decades of experience as the leader of the Methodist revival, he wrote in his journal:

> I was more convinced than ever that the preaching like an apostle, without joining together those that are awakened and training them up in the ways of God, is only begetting children for the murderer. How much preaching has there been for these twenty years all over Pembrokeshire? But no *regular* societies, no discipline, no order or connection. And the consequence is that nine in ten of the awakened are now faster asleep than ever.[12]

Wesley did not seem puzzled or even surprised by the state of affairs, but offered a direct and straightforward diagnosis of the problem. Those who had been awakened were subsequently in an even worse state because they had not been joined together in groups.

---

11. Taken from *The Works of John Wesley, Vol 14*, "Preface," and "Hymns and Sacred Poems," by John Wesley, copyright © 1984 by John Wesley. Used by permission of Zondervan.

12. Taken from *The Works of John Wesley, Vol 14*, "*Journal* for August 25, 1763, in *Works, 21*," by John Wesley. Copyright © 1984 by John Wesley. Used by permission of Zondervan.

The Giving Tree

Contemporary scholarship, encumbered as it is with the very debates for which Wesley held such distaste, has obscured the core legacy of John Wesley. The goal of the Christian life, according to John Wesley, was holiness. Holiness, in his view, was only achievable in the context of community. In other words, Christianity was a matter of action, of a life lived differently than the world. All of this was accomplished by grace through faith within the Christian congregation context, where there was mutual accountability, transparency, and support. To achieve this end, John Wesley utilized a small-group structure consisting primarily of Methodist bands and classes. While these two groups were differentiated somewhat, they shared the common goal of facilitating holiness, which was expressed in the love of God and neighbor in the context of mutual accountability.

There is much academic discussion as to which small group was the most important, the class or the band. In addition, some claim the class to be an original contribution of Wesley and thus of Methodism to the Christian landscape. Wesley's beliefs should be taken in context. In doing so, it becomes clear that Wesley's band and class structure—his structure for discipleship—has its roots in a long history of house groups, beginning in the first-century Roman Empire and extending to the present worldwide house church movement. To state the origination point of the Methodist small groups was not with John Wesley is not to undercut their significance, but rather to increase it by placing them within the Christian legacy originating in the first century.

Wesley was deeply committed to correct doctrine because it provided guidelines for right living. He was equally committed to the pursuit of holiness in the context of small groups. These discipleship groups were what Wesley viewed as the sinews of Methodist society. He stated:

> Never omit meeting your Class or Band. These are the very sinews of our Society; and whatever weakens or tends to weaken our regard for these, or our exactness in attending them, strikes at the very root of our community.[13]

---
13. Kevin Watson, *The Class Meeting: Reclaiming a Forgotten (and Essential) Small Group Experience* (Franklin, TN: Seedbed, 2013), 19.

Transformed by Love

John Wesley was a key leader in the eighteenth-century Evangelical Revival. He was preaching to "reform the nation," particularly the church, and to "spread scriptural holiness throughout the land."[14] His goal wasn't just to awaken people to their need for salvation but also to cast a vision for the Christian life. The method consisted not of the form of the classes or bands but of what transpired within them. Wesley's approach to social holiness provided intimacy and a sense of belonging in the era of social displacement that coincided with the advent of industrialization in England. The class and band meetings were the places where the Methodist message went from print to voice, from thought to action, from individual to community.

The purpose of these groups was not merely to ensure the Methodists were not hypocrites, but to facilitate genuine care for one another so that they would begin bearing one another's burdens and watching over each other in love. Wesley had observed that when the continuing work of grace was taken for granted, there was a falling away—even by the most mature Christians. In other words, the Christian life was one of moment-by-moment conscious obedience. For Wesley, therefore, Christian discipleship's greatest question was how to foster an environment where God's grace could do unhindered sanctifying work in the believer. His solution was to place believers in groups where they could learn to love, share their experiences and burdens, and enter into mutual accountability for that discipleship. Irrespective of their differing constitutions, both the band and the class meetings' primary aim was to facilitate growth in one's relationship with God. In the context of these meetings, Methodists were asked to live transparently, invite others into their lives, and to be involved deeply in the lives of others so together they could grow in grace.

Wesley brought together two strands from his own experience: the Anglican understanding of the importance of a disciplined practice of the means of grace for growth in holiness, and the Moravian understanding of the need for justification by faith and the witness of the Spirit.

---

14. Kevin Watson, *The Class Meeting: Reclaiming a Forgotten (and Essential) Small Group Experience* (Franklin, TN: Seedbed, 2013), 7.

The Giving Tree

Methodists were expected to read their Bibles, attend public worship, pray consistently, fast, and partake of the Lord's Supper. Adherence to these practices was a requirement of the General Rules. At the same time, Wesley believed that faith must be personal, so he emphasized the importance of the individual's encounter with the Holy Spirit.

The essence of the class and band meetings was prayer and sharing about personal experiences with God. This seemed to draw the Holy Spirit, and many came to saving faith in Jesus Christ in the context of the class meetings. A strong case can be made that the class and band meetings were the single most important factor in the explosive growth of Methodism and the retention of members. New converts to Methodism were immediately placed in classes where they would be discipled and learn to practice their faith.

Even more revealing as to the underlying reason for the efficacy of these groups consists of what they were not. These groups were not Bible studies. They were not information-driven groups whose aim was to acquire more intellectual knowledge about faith. They did not have a set curriculum or engage in the study of any book about the Christian journey. They did not entail the transfer of information from one person, the pastor or leader, to a group of passive consumers. These groups were alive and dynamic families of living faith with each member as equally engaged as all of the others in learning to walk in grace, learning to love, all in the context of the community. In short, they were engaged in biblical discipleship.

***

Helen

Helen was a woman in need of a miracle. She was literally on her deathbed when a friend called to ask whether I would go pray for her. She was in a cancer hospice. Helen was unconscious when we entered the room. The hospital staff, her family, and her friends had already accepted that she would die soon and had made arrangements in accordance with that expectation. Helen's friend and I prayed in her room. I sang and praised the Lord in her room as the hospital staff walked in and out, trying not to disturb us. The words I kept hearing from the Lord were that he wanted "to redeem her whole life." I proclaimed those repeatedly. After approximately thirty minutes, we kissed Helen on the forehead and left the hospice.

A couple of days passed. I received a phone call from a number I did not recognize. It was Helen. She was completely healed physically and was making plans for her future! She even made a video for her family, which displayed not only her physical healing, but a new attitude. The hospital staff was so startled at the abrupt and complete change in her that they thought another patient had been mistakenly put in her room.

I wish with all of my heart that the ending to Helen's story would have been the fulfillment of all of her dreams, but it was not. Pasquale and I sought to find her a place to live and get her started in her new life, but it was challenging. We were not close to her geographically, were not her pastors, and could not provide the continuing care and support she needed. Without the necessary support and guidance, Helen eventually sank back into a very dark and lonely place. Despite the miraculous physical healing she received, the healing she needed for her broken heart never happened. Consequently, the "redemption of her whole life," which I had heard from the Holy Spirit, was never brought to fruition.

Helen's story was not a "success" for the kingdom, in my view. It did not bring God everlasting glory, but it did teach me the value of covenant relationships between believers. I believe that Helen did not experience her complete healing because of a lack of Christian family and support in the body of Christ. Helen, despite her status as a child of God, was alone. Church is not a place or a destination. Church was meant to be a family of believers and the body of Christ. Programs, studies, and activities can never replace the relationships which are the heart and soul of the church. Jesus both demonstrated and taught what it means to have love expressed by a willingness to lay our lives down on behalf of another. Love is the heart of the covenant relationship.

***

The Giving Tree

John Wesley: A Voice for the Ages

Toward the end of his life, in an essay on Methodism's future, John Wesley wrote that Methodism would have a bright future so long as it held fast to both Methodist teaching about God and Methodist practice of meeting in the classes and bands. Wesley wrote:

> I am not afraid that the people called Methodists should ever cease to exist either in Europe or America. But I am afraid lest they should exist as a dead sect, having the form of religion without the power. And this undoubtedly will be the case unless they hold fast both the doctrine, spirit, and discipline with which they first set out.[15]

From the above quote, it's clear that John Wesley valued both the Methodist message and method, and considered them essential to Methodism's continuing vitality. Unfortunately, academic scholarship has largely overlooked Wesley's true genius and thus his relevance for our time by becoming bogged down in the intellectual debates for which Wesley showed such aversion. The twenty-first-century church in America desperately needs the very reform which John Wesley brought to the church of his time.

The term "holiness" for most theologians and ordinary Christians alike is a slippery term, the meaning of which the mind seems unable to grasp. However, the message of Methodism (radical as it was—and still is) was certainly not new. In essence, John Wesley was preaching the message of love, and that the Christian journey was one of learning how to love. By learning how to love, one was formed increasingly into the likeness of Jesus Christ. John Wesley was and is a radical voice for the ages because he dared to believe that Jesus was serious in his Sermon on the Mount. The Beatitudes, therefore, were not an unattainable theoretical ideal for an unidentifiable time in the future, but were the paradigm for kingdom living in the present. The "Methodist message," therefore,

---

15. Kevin Watson, *The Class Meeting: Reclaiming a Forgotten (and Essential) Small Group Experience*, (Franklin, TN: Seedbed, 2013), 36.

has been obscured and Wesley's witness muted by both ignorance and misunderstanding. John Wesley's witness, which lit both England and America on fire, was the voice that casts a vision of a kingdom reality in the here and now and calls all would-be disciples into that vision. This is the true legacy of John Wesley.

The "Methodist Method" has also been lost in academic discussions of classes versus bands and the original contribution of Methodism. At the risk of offending every Methodist, neither classes nor bands were an original contribution of Methodism. The reality is that every disciple of Jesus Christ was first discipled by someone else. John Wesley was discipled by his mother, Susanna Wesley, a devout Christian. Susanna Wesley suffered extreme hardship during her lifetime, including the death of nine of her nineteen children, financial hardship, and physical illness. Her life's main goal was to unite her family and see her children's souls saved. She was so devoted to this mission that she ordered her life around discipling her ten living children, and would set aside one hour each day for a particular child, taking time to ask them about the state of his or her soul. This regular self-examination and mutual accountability were the seeds for the classes and were echoed in the question that was the focus of every class meeting: How does your soul prosper?

As recent studies have underscored the value of small groups, churches have rushed to start small groups, but Wesley was not creating small groups. The efficacy of the Methodist method was not in the fact that the groups were small. Small groups can be equally as ineffective and disjointed as large ones if they are information-driven. Rather ironically, Methodist classes were all but gone at the beginning of the twentieth century due to their replacement by other small groups—Bible studies and Sunday school classes.

In fact, it is quite sobering to contemplate the notion that Wesley was advocating the small group. It is also absurd to think of God as advocating the small group. John Wesley was preaching justification by faith alone and the witness of the Spirit who declares one to be a child of God. As children of God, believers did not become simply members of a class or band—they became family. God was creating a family in Jesus Christ. Thus, drawing on Scripture as well as his own natural family, John Wesley was creating a setting where believers could become disciples in the context of a loving and supportive family.

In the final analysis, neither the message nor the method of Methodism was truly novel. Instead, John Wesley was a radical voice harking back to the roots of biblical discipleship. In his day, as in ours, the church has carefully fostered the notion that there is a category of belief that does not require following Jesus. In other words, no transformation is required. The nominal Christian life has become the norm, and the abundant Christian life a pipedream. As in John Wesley's time, the church as a whole is "almost Christian," and the Christian witness has gone silent. The emperor has no clothes.

The influence of the American church is not forever lost. The answer may just be found in some of the treasures hidden in the message and method of John Wesley. There we rediscover truths that go back to Jesus and his first disciples. This includes the reality that Christianity is a lifelong journey of a partnership between human free will and God's grace. It is where each believer learns to grow in the love of God and neighbor, where the individual is transformed, and that transformation, in turn, affects others. This transformation takes place in the community, in the family of believers, where self-examination, transparency, and intimacy are present so Christians can watch over one another in love. Once again, a vision must be cast that the Beatitudes are possible, following Jesus is not optional, and the kingdom must be ushered into the here and now. This is not only the most excellent way, but it is also the only way to restore the voice of the Christian witness to the American church.

5

Called to Be a Witness

Song of the Bride

Many and varied are the accusations leveled at the American church of the twenty-first century. According to her critics, she is powerless, unchristlike, divided, hypocritical, judgmental, and mostly irrelevant—all at the same time. To a large extent, these claims are substantiated by statistical evidence. A number of recent studies suggest that Americans believe religion—Christianity included—is losing influence. The church has lost its authoritative voice. The consensus appears to be that the church, in her present state, is ineffective in influencing culture. The American church seems to exist either in ignorance or denial of Jesus' commission to "Go and make disciples of all nations…teaching them to obey everything I have commanded you" (Matthew 28:19-20). What will the future of it be?

Successful people typically begin a new venture with the end in mind. The destination casts a vision for the entire journey. It is common business practice for corporations to craft both mission and vision statements to ensure they achieve their desired objectives. The vision and the mission are the "end," which is always kept in focus. Many churches have adopted a quasi-corporate governance style, crafting their own unique vision and mission statements. This may seem to make intrinsic sense to a Christian church immersed in secular culture and permeated

The Giving Tree

by the things of the world, but a multiplicity of visions and a plethora of missions suggest both the possibility and the acceptability of deviation by the church of Christ from the mission and vision of Christ.

For the church to move beyond nominal Christianity, the vision Jesus cast for his church in Scripture must be restored. The book of Revelation contains the truth about the end of the story. It is the final chapter and the definitive statement of the destiny of his church. The vision of Jesus for his church is a spotless bride clothed in white linen. This is her destiny and it is, therefore, the destiny of the American church.

> Let us rejoice and be glad and give him glory! For the wedding of the Lamb has come, and his bride has made herself ready. Fine linen, bright and clean, was given her to wear. (Fine linen stands for the righteous acts of God's holy people.) (Revelation 19:7-8)

Americans are often accused by those from other cultures of being overly enamored with the idea of a "happy ending." In fact, no film and no story seem truly complete without it. No matter what twists and turns a storyline or a movie plot may take—regardless of the intensity of the evil resident in the villain or the ineptness of the protagonists—Americans are virtually assured that the tables will turn and a happy ending will be secured. Fortunately, there is a happy ending in store for the church, the bride of Christ, who will not be found wanting at the return of Jesus. She will have made herself ready. This is the vision for the church and her future. Such a glorious destiny should silence the critics who have deemed her too backslidden to be relevant.

In order to guide her into that destiny, however, the biblical view of her identity and her mission must be recaptured. In Western thinking, the term *church* has, unfortunately, become synonymous with a place, a building, and a destination; church is a place to go, an activity. Nothing could be further from the truth. The word *church* isn't about a building or place, but rather people coming together to fulfill a common purpose. In other words, *church* isn't referring to a destination at all, but the assembled believers themselves. In fact, the Bible states the church, the house of God, is comprised of believers who are themselves the living stones out of which the house is made.

> As you come to him, the living Stone—rejected by humans but chosen by God and precious to him—you also, like living stones, are being built into a spiritual house to be a holy priesthood, offering spiritual sacrifices acceptable to God through Jesus Christ. (1 Peter 2:4-5)

The church of Jesus Christ, according to Scripture, is not an institution, nor is it a corporate-like entity. Quite the contrary, it is a living organism comprised of believers. It is the bride of Christ. Consequently, her preparedness as a "spiritual house" is only equivalent to the preparedness of the constituent "living stones" out of which the house is constructed.

If the vision for the church is a spotless bride prepared for her husband, then of what does her mission consist? In the opening chapters of the book of Revelation, Jesus addressed the church as a whole, the so-called church universal, symbolized by seven different churches. These churches are called out by geographical location. In fact, the book of Acts is replete with references to churches all based on geographical location. In sharp contrast are the existing dividing lines in the contemporary church which have arisen largely as the result of doctrinal disputes. This is the church from an earthly vantage point. Is it possible that heaven does not agree, but sweeps aside doctrinal separations as insignificant, instead viewing the church as unified based on the notion of land?

The emphasis on land and its occupation is, in fact, more consistent with the divine mandate to take dominion over the land as found in the opening chapters of Genesis (see Genesis 1:28). Even more, the subject of land (which was promised to Abraham and his descendants) is one of the major themes found throughout the Pentateuch. What would be the implications for the individual believer and for the American church as a whole if God's placement in this particular land was, indeed, purposeful, intentional, and timely? According to the statements of Paul in the book of Acts, God determines the exact place and time each person lives.

> From one man he made all the nations, that they should inhabit the whole earth; and he marked out their appointed times in history and the boundaries of their lands. God did this so that they would seek him and perhaps reach out for him and find him, though he is not far from any one of us. (Acts 17:26-27)

The biblical emphasis on land and geographical location requires a paradigm-shift in the Christian mindset. American believers need a shift in their thinking. They need a new paradigm. If God purposefully planned both the time and place for each believer, then the destiny of each would be inextricably tied to the land. By extension, the church's placement in a particular land would also be intentional, and its mission geographically significant. In particular, the role of each individual believer, and that of the church as a whole, would be to partner with God in extending his dominion over the land.

***

Taking Dominion

As believers and children of God, we are under a divine mandate to take dominion over the square foot of earth on which we are standing. This is never more apparent than when we pray over houses, buildings, or land. Our team is the only team in our area, to my knowledge, which goes out regularly to pray over houses, churches, and buildings. On this particular occasion, a pastor called us on behalf of some of her congregants who were experiencing bizarre occurrences in their home. Their children were being awakened in the night and tormented. The parents would find marks on their children's bodies that could not be explained. Terrified, the children did not want to remain in the house.

Called to Be a Witness

We agreed to come and pray over the house. The history of the house was unknown to the occupants, as it had been a rental property. When we arrived, the Holy Spirit instructed us to have worship music in the house. I requested that the owners turn on worship music. The entire electrical system in the house, which had been working properly up to that moment, inexplicably failed. I looked up to heaven and asked, "Now what, Lord? There is no worship music."

I heard him answer clearly, "You worship. You are the worship music. Sing."

Now anyone who knows me well would know that I would be the last person to begin belting out a song in front of strangers. The Holy Spirit was insistent, so I began to sing and worship the Lord. In fact, I sang for hours as Pasquale and the team prayed through the house. The Lord revealed that the house had a history of owners who had abused their children. We prayed for cleansing, covering everything in the blood of Jesus. We repented on behalf of the previous occupants for the atrocities committed there.

Through it all, I sang. I sang of the glory of God, of all of his wonders, and of his goodness. I gave him praise and honor. After half a day had passed, exhausted, we felt we were finished. The Lord then instructed us to pray for the family. We began to pray for the family, and God began to work miracles of healing and restoration. The people who were healed began calling their friends, relatives, and neighbors, and a full healing service began in this home that had been dedicated to the Lord.

We received a card from them a few months later. There had been no more incidents of any kind in the home since we prayed, and a sense of peace had been restored to both the immediate family and the extended family. The news of what God had done in the house and with the family had traveled throughout the neighborhood.

***

This land called America is, therefore, the mission field for every American believer who is called to take dominion over it. In effect, American Christians are missionaries to and in America—now that requires a radical paradigm-shift! This shift in paradigm would bring the American church into line with her biblical mandate. The church has a mission statement—the mission statement of Jesus Christ. Jesus came to "seek and save the lost" (Luke 19:10) which fulfills the desire of the Father who doesn't want "anyone to perish but everyone to come to repentance" (2 Peter 3:9).

This paradigm-shift also involves a shift in thinking about the necessity for sharing the gospel. One of the often misquoted, misguided, and misplaced justifications for not sharing the gospel is the erroneous view that it can be preached without words. The purported unbiblical supremacy of actions over words has infiltrated the church as justification for silence and is often attributed to Francis of Assisi who is quoted as having said, "Preach the gospel at all times. When necessary, use words." As far as can be ascertained, Francis never said this. His actual words were, "It is no use walking anywhere to preach unless our walking is our preaching...As for me, I desire this privilege from the Lord, that never may I have any privilege from man, except to do reverence to all, and to convert the world by obedience to the Holy Rule rather by example than by word."

Francis, in fact, was deeply committed to both the verbal proclamation and the practice of the gospel in daily life. In order to be properly understood, the above quote must be taken in its context. Francis' main audience was made up of nominal Christians whose lives did not reflect their beliefs. His saying was a context-specific correction and never intended to elevate actions over words. In fact, it would be a glaring oxymoron to assert that Jesus, who is called the Word, would ever suggest that his gospel could or should be shared without words.

The American church needs to find her words, find her voice, and fulfill her mission. The bride of Christ has a song, a sound, as it were. She sounds "like a great multitude, like the roar of rushing waters, and like loud peals of thunder" (Revelation 19:6). As will be explained further in the chapters to come, that sound, the song of the bride, is the very sound of God.

Called to Be a Witness

The True Christian Witness

If church is not a place, not an activity, and not a destination, but consists instead of holy habitation constructed from the individual believers as living stones, believers today must have an identity and a purpose distinct from and not confined to the four walls of a building. During his earthly ministry, Jesus sent the disciples out two by two with specific instructions.

> When Jesus had called the Twelve together, he gave them power and authority to drive out all demons and to cure diseases, and he sent them out to proclaim the kingdom of God and to heal the sick. (Luke 9:1-2)

Thus, the disciples were sent out specifically to witness to the truth of the coming of the kingdom of God by proclamation (word) and by demonstration (deed). After his death and resurrection, Jesus appeared to the disciples and remained with them forty days teaching about the kingdom of heaven. He then told them about the baptism of the Holy Spirit, which would give them power to be his witnesses:

> But you will receive power when the Holy Spirit comes on you; and you will be my witnesses in Jerusalem, and in all Judea and Samaria, and to the ends of the earth. (Acts 1:8)

Imagine the surprise on the face of the contemporary church-going Christian in America at the discovery that he or she has been called, summoned, and sent out as a witness to testify on behalf of Jesus. Incredulous at the implication that the average Christian is actually called to present evidence on Jesus' behalf, an inner voice might protest against a role reserved exclusively for "evangelists." According to Scripture, Jesus did not choose some to be witnesses, but sent all without exception to share the gospel. A specific calling to evangelism was not required, sinless perfection was not required, nor was a seminary education. The single prerequisite was faith. Without faith, there can be no witness for faith, which lies at the heart of the Christian witness.

The biblical concept of "witness" is, in fact, a legal term. Thus, there are many applicable analogies from the secular courtroom. The role of a witness in the contemporary courtroom is helpful in illuminating the role of the Christian witness. Courtroom scenes and courtroom drama are frequently played out in both the media and on television. Therefore, the role of a witness in a secular courtroom is relatively familiar to the majority of people, even in the absence of personal experience with the judicial system. Simply stated, a witness is a person called by one of the parties to a legal proceeding to give verbal evidence on that party's behalf. This evidence is called "testimony."

In any court proceeding, witness testimony can be an important source of evidence. Consequently, courts take being called as a witness very seriously. In fact, witnesses who refuse to testify can, in some situations, be held in contempt of court, which may result in penalties, including fines and imprisonment. The weight of the witness' testimony depends on its credibility or how the judge or jury perceives its truthfulness. One of the determinants of credibility is whether the witness had the opportunity to personally see or hear the events contained in the testimony. Another major factor in establishing credibility is the character of the witness, particularly in regard to truthfulness.

The Sound of Faith

The first element of the commission Jesus gave to his disciples was "to proclaim the kingdom of God." Drawing from the secular courtroom, the weight or believability of their testimony was directly proportional and utterly dependent on their "ability to see or hear the events" contained in the testimony. The gospel of John, in particular, emphasizes the twin themes of witness and testimony, with such references far outnumbering other Gospel accounts. The gospel of John, in fact, hinges its reliability on eyewitness testimony of those with personal knowledge of Jesus. Emphasis on eyewitness testimony is used in John's gospel account as a type of "bookend" which begins, ends, and holds the entire account together. The first eyewitness mentioned is John the Baptist.

> There was a man sent from God whose name was John. He came as a witness to testify concerning that light, so that through him all might believe. He himself was not the light; he came only as a witness to the light. (John 1:6-8)

The apostle John ends his account with an affirmation of the truth of his own eyewitness testimony.

> This is the disciple who testifies to these things and who wrote them down. We know that his testimony is true. Jesus did many other things as well. If every one of them were written down, I suppose that even the whole world would not have room for the books that would be written. (John 21:24-25)

The purpose of John's gospel is expressly stated in the text, "That you may believe that Jesus is the Christ, the Son of God, and by believing you may have life in his name" (John 20:31). In other words, the purpose of John's testimony is to bear witness to the true identity of Jesus as the Messiah and, thus, to bring others to faith and life in Jesus. Jesus came to seek and save that which was lost. John shares the mission of Jesus, as does each and every believer who has found new life in Christ. This is the role of the Christian witness. The credibility of that witness, as in the secular courtroom and as reflected in the gospel of John, depends on personal experience. The Christian witness devoid of credibility only serves to create confusion among nonbelievers as to the true nature of Christ.

To serve as a credible witness and to "proclaim the kingdom of God" requires personal knowledge. Personal knowledge can only be gained through personal experience. It may be shocking to discover the idea that eyewitness testimony from personal experience with the God of the Bible (who is still very much alive) is not only possible, but at the very center of what it means to have faith. In fact, in the absence of firsthand knowledge of God, there can be no faith, only religion. Perhaps the most critical factor in restoring the true Christian witness is the restoration of faith. It is noteworthy that "faith" does not even appear as one of the topics in many theology books, perhaps because it is considered too rudimentary to justify scholarly commentary. If it is so rudimentary, thus rendering its discussion superfluous, then why do so many Christians lament its lack? In light of the fact that many Christians admit to struggling with it, nonbelievers need it, and the Bible tells us we cannot please God without it (Hebrews 11:6), faith demands a second look.

Whatever this elusive quality called "faith" is, Christians cannot do without it. Abraham is said to have had it, as did both Noah and Moses. On the other hand, Jesus often rebuked his disciples for having too little of it. The single common denominator in all of the failures of God's people has always been a lack of faith.

So what exactly is faith, and how does one get more of it?

Prior to his death, Jesus exhorted his disciples to "believe," or to have faith. "Do not let your hearts be troubled. You believe in God; believe also in me" (John 14:1). The word translated as "believe" has its origin in Greek from a root word meaning "to bind," for example, as in a contract. In the contemporary legal field, a contract meeting all legal prerequisites is called a "binding" contract because it binds the two parties of the contract to its terms and the mutual promises which they have made to each other. This "binding" of the two parties together consists not just of the mutual assent to the contract, but also mandates action as outlined in the contract. The parties are thus bound to each other for the length of the contract and until the terms of the agreement have been fulfilled. From this perspective, Jesus is telling his disciples to "bind themselves" to him.

Jon Ruthven, in his book *What's Wrong with Protestant Theology,* presents a very thorough examination of what constitutes biblical faith, concluding that faith can be defined as "hearing the immediate word of

God and responding appropriately."[16] This type of faith cries out for the addition of the dynamic and colorful qualities exemplified by real faith. Certainly faith is obedient, but it is at the same time courageous, bold, alive, and unpredictable. In fact, faith defies a linear and logical definition which is one-dimensional. Faith is multi-dimensional. Faith requires more than a definition. It demands an illustration, a portrait, a story. Biblical figures who embodied faith were truly friends of God and exhibited traits which were both radical and courageous. True faith is a motivator of epic proportion, which moves people to color outside the lines and challenge the status quo. In his parables about faith, Jesus illustrated these qualities.

In examining the parables of Jesus, Brad Young suggests that the faith in Jesus' parables, particularly the Friend at Midnight (Luke 11:5-8) and the Persistent Widow (Luke 18:1-8), could be compared to the Hebrew word *Chutzpah*. *Chutzpah* means "headstrong persistence, brazen impudence, bold determination, unyielding tenacity, or raw nerve."[17] The persistent widow appeared unaccompanied before the unjust judge repeatedly in a culture and time where women had no voice and no right to speak on their own behalf. From a legal standpoint, she was required to have a man speak for her. Yet she appeared without status, without a male voice, without money, and without influence. The only resource she possessed was sheer tenacity. This widow, according to Jesus, exemplified true faith. Jesus concluded the parable with a question regarding faith, a question which should resound in contemporary Christian ears: "However, when the Son of Man comes will he find faith on earth?" (Luke 18:8).

Religion raises its voice in objection to *Chutzpah,* citing breach of proper etiquette. "Surely, it says, no one should ever approach God in such a fashion." The voice of faith declares otherwise. In fact, Jewish

---

16. Jon Mark Ruthven, *What's Wrong with Protestant Theology: Tradition vs. Biblical Emphasis* (Tulsa, OK, Word & Spirit Press, 2013), 136.

17. *Jesus the Jewish Theologian* by Brad H. Young, copyright 1995 by Hendrickson Publishers, Peabody, Massachusetts. Used by permission. All rights reserved.

rabbis had a high regard for *Chutzpah* as a valid expression of faith.[18] Abraham, whom God called his friend, both argued and negotiated with God. Abraham was but the first in a long line of people with *Chutzpah*, all of whom enjoyed a close relationship with God. Jacob wrestled with God for a blessing and was later renamed "Israel." When God declared his intention to destroy the people of Israel for worshipping the golden calf, Moses pleaded with God to reconsider.

During Jesus' earthly ministry, it was precisely this brazenness, this *Chutzpah,* which captured his attention, and which Jesus commended as faith. It was the people with unrelenting persistence who had their requests granted. The woman with the issue of blood was driven by her faith to do the unimaginable, pressing through the crowd despite her uncleanness to gain her healing by touching the Rabbi Jesus' prayer shawl (Luke 8:44). The faith of the paralytic's friends refused to be deterred by their inability to enter through the front door of the house to get to Jesus, so they tore off the roof and lowered him down instead (Luke 5:17-19). The Canaanite woman begged Jesus to heal her daughter, persisting even in the face of Jesus' initial refusal and apparent rudeness (Matthew 15:22-28).

Biblical faith is not merely the intellectual assent to a creed or a specific set of beliefs, but consists rather of binding oneself to God, with a commitment to never let go. Ruth bound herself to Naomi, and in doing so, bound herself to Naomi's God.

> But Ruth replied, "Don't urge me to leave you or to turn back from you. Where you go I will go, and where you stay I will stay. Your people will be my people and your God my God. Where you die I will die, and there I will be buried. May the Lord deal with me, be it ever so severely, if even death separates you and me." (Ruth 1:16-17)

---

18. *Jesus the Jewish Theologian* by Brad H. Young, copyright 1995 by Hendrickson Publishers, Peabody, Massachusetts. Used by permission. All rights reserved.

Called to Be a Witness

This covenant relationship, this binding of oneself to God is the essence of faith. From the very beginning, God has always been unwavering in his intention for people to have a relationship with him. The promise of relationship is one of three major promises of the Pentateuch, along with land and descendants.

Like faith, the topic of new covenant relationship may appear too obvious to merit serious academic discussion. Lawyers, however, take great pride in stating the obvious. Only a courageous voice would dare to risk the disdain of others by asking whether contemporary church-going Christians truly understand that God desires a personal relationship with each of his children. In other words, do contemporary Christians understand that the essence of the new covenant is more than a momentary recitation of the sinner's prayer? If one were to judge by the typical Sunday fare served up for consumption—a menu of announcements, a presentation of biblical reasons why Christians should give money to the church, followed by the main course of an entertaining sermon, little room has been left for God. Perhaps the obvious is not quite so obvious after all.

Faith is the assurance that God will never let go of us. This is the essence of faith—to know, regardless of circumstances, that God is present. The success of Moses' impossible mission to deliver the Israelites out of Egyptian bondage was assured by one fact—God was going to be with him. "I will be with you" (Exodus 3:12). It was during the commissioning of Moses that God revealed his personal covenant name, "I AM who I AM" (Exodus 3:14).

The conjunction for "who" can also be translated as to where something is located.[19] Translated with "where," the divine name would be rendered "I AM where I AM," further emphasizing the fact that God, who is omnipresent, can and does choose to be manifestly present in a particular place with a particular person. In this case, God assured Moses of success because he (God) was going with him. Moses may

---

19. "H1961 - hayah - Strong's Hebrew Lexicon (KJV)." Blue Letter Bible. Accessed 1 Feb, 2021. https://www.blueletterbible.org//lang/lexicon/lexicon.cfm?Strongs=H1961&t=KJV

have grappled with this notion at his initial encounter with God, but he later realized its full implications. Moses understood not only that success was guaranteed by God's presence, but also that God's presence was the distinguishing feature which set the Israelites apart.

> The Lord replied, "My Presence will go with you, and I will give you rest."
>
> Then Moses said to him, "If your Presence does not go with us, do not send us up from here. How will anyone know that you are pleased with me and with your people unless you go with us? What else will distinguish me and your people from all the other people on the face of the earth?" (Exodus 33:14-16)

Jesus uttered similar words to his disciples when he commissioned them.

> Therefore go and make disciples of all nations, baptizing them in the name of the Father and of the Son and of the Holy Spirit, and teaching them to obey everything I have commanded you. And surely I am with you always, to the very end of the age. (Matthew 28:19-20)

Jesus echoed the promise made to Moses, guaranteeing the success of the disciples' mission by his presence with them.

Certainly faith is comprised of obedience, an appropriate response to hearing the word of God, but faith is also dynamic, alive, and courageous. It is the substance that causes ordinary human beings to rise up, bind themselves to an extraordinary God, and release a sound—a tribute to the goodness of God. That sound is the sound of heaven. It is the sound of the child of God, crying out "Abba, Father." This sound declares, "Even though I walk through the darkest valley, I will fear no evil, for you are with me" (Psalm 23:4). This sound brings heaven to earth!

***

Called to Be a Witness

The Coronavirus Pandemic

March of 2020 was like no other in recent history. We felt as if we had been blindsided, punched in the gut as it were. Completely unprepared, the COVID-19 pandemic took New York City and the surrounding area by storm. The hospitals were unprepared, the people were unprepared—and the church was unprepared.

The last weeks of February had been spent with busy preparations for our yearly fundraiser, which I preferred to think of as a community celebration. My heart had never been truly invested in such activities, as I strongly prefer to expend my energy and attention on the mission field. On my way back home from one of the planning meetings, the Holy Spirit, asked me, "Is your trust in me or in your fundraiser?"

Sensing that perhaps I had become a little too dependent on the yearly fundraiser, I knew what the answer should be. "My trust is in you, Lord, please forgive me if I have placed it elsewhere."

Less than one week later, our fundraiser had been cancelled. In fact, all fundraisers had been cancelled and life as we know it had been put on hold. The Coronavirus had turned everything upside down and the rules had changed. Hunkered down in their houses not knowing what to expect, people were afraid and began to amass quantities of necessities. Out of fear, they began hoarding food, water, toilet paper, and other necessities. Businesses closed and jobs were lost.

At our food pantry, lines lengthened and we began to see increasing numbers of people from all walks of life line up for food. The churches had closed, as well as a number of other area food pantries. Not knowing what else to do, we remained open and reorganized to maintain safety and relative order. For the first time, we faced food shortages. The food from food rescue, which had always been more than enough, had dropped to a bare minimum. Food hoarding by those with resources had now affected the supplies for those living on the edge.

"Lord, what do we do?" I asked in desperation.

"Ask the community," he said.

We put out a brief request out on social media, telling of our need. What followed was astonishing. There was an instant outpouring in the community of food, finances, and help. In the midst of trouble and hardship, the Lord brought blessing. Clergy rallied their congregations to gather food. Businesses partnered with us to give finances and support. Even the schools donated their leftover food.

"What is your plan for the future?" we were often asked.

"God is our plan," I would respond. "There is no other plan."

To some, that might seem irresponsible. To me, it seemed just right. God proved himself faithful in the most difficult of times. Trust in a fundraiser? I think not.

***

Belief in the Goodness of God Required

At times it seems the notion of faith takes on a life of its own, independent of its object. Christian faith is not placed in faith, but God is the true object of faith. Faith may find its definition in Ruthven's "hearing the word of God and responding" and its expression in bold persistence, but it must be predicated on a belief in the inherent goodness of God. After all, why would anyone wish to hear, much less obey a god whose motives and objectives were not good? The type of faith that perseveres under duress and is unrelenting in the face of severe hardship has as its prerequisite an underlying belief in God's goodness.

In the past few years, much has been written and produced about the fact that "God is not dead." However, the problem may not be a question regarding God's existence, but rather that he has been forgotten. If God has been forgotten, then the problem must lie in one of two areas: either there is a conspiracy of silence among believers, or the Christian witness is no longer credible. A person called as a witness must, by definition, give a testimony as evidence, for that is the very reason a witness is called. Imagine the rather odd scenario in which a lawyer calls a witness, puts him or her on the witness stand in front of the jury, simply waits a few minutes while the witness sits in silence, and then summarily dismisses the witness without a word. What would be the reaction of the jury? Such a situation would cause immense confusion, for a silent witness is no witness at all.

Called to Be a Witness

Jesus sent his disciples out to "proclaim the kingdom of God." The kingdom of God is the sovereign reign and rule of God, which was foretold by Old Testament prophets and was ushered in with the ministry of Jesus. The reign of any ruler reflects his or her character and nature. Thus, the reign of God reflects his character and nature. In the Old Testament, the people of Israel were God's witnesses (Isaiah 43:10; 44:8-9). They were called to testify to his uniqueness, love, mercy, power, and holiness. God himself serves as the greatest witness in the Bible, often testifying on his own behalf.

In the Old Testament, judicial procedure mandated that a matter could only be established on the testimony of two or three witnesses (Deuteronomy 17:6; 19:15). This principle was an integral part of Jewish law which continued into the New Testament "Every matter must be established by the testimony of two or three witnesses" (2 Corinthians 13:1; see also Matthew 18:16). The testimony of the two or three witnesses must be in agreement, of course, to establish the matter. In the case of the proclamation of the kingdom of God, the Christian witness must agree with the witness God provides about himself. At one point, Moses requested that God show him his glory. The Lord responded to Moses, "I will cause all my goodness to pass in front of you, and I will proclaim my name, the Lord, in your presence" (Exodus 33:19). Moses' request was a simple if outrageous one—to gaze upon the glory of the Lord. God agreed. However, he insisted that it be accompanied by the proclamation of his character or nature. God did not pass by Moses in silence, but gave witness to his own name.

> Then the Lord came down in the cloud and stood there with him and proclaimed his name, the Lord. And he passed in front of Moses, proclaiming, "The Lord, the Lord, the compassionate and gracious God, slow to anger, abounding in love and faithfulness, maintaining love to thousands, and forgiving wickedness, rebellion and sin. Yet he does not leave the guilty unpunished; he punishes

the children and their children for the sin of the parents to the third and fourth generation." (Ex. 34:5-7)

The Lord told Moses he would cause his "goodness" to pass in front of him. That goodness or glory was accompanied by a simultaneous proclamation of his attributes—compassion, grace, faithfulness, mercy, and holiness. Jesus sent his disciples out to proclaim the coming of God's rule on earth. The proclamation was to be accompanied by demonstration—healing the sick, driving out demons, and raising the dead. The true Christian witness is the testimony that corroborates the witness God has already given about himself. The true Christian witness has a sound, and that sound is a tribute to the goodness of God.

The book of Psalms consists largely of the testimony of David regarding the goodness of God through all circumstances. The Psalms remain a lasting legacy for generations of Christians. David's Psalms resound throughout the ages, a testimony of what it means to have faith, to bind oneself to God, a God who is faithful, compassionate, and above all, good. It resounds with the tonality of a true witness, declaring that God is a God who is with his people. "I cling to you; your right hand upholds me" (Psalm 63:8). David, indeed, enjoyed an intimate relationship with the Lord, heard him, and obeyed him. David testified to the goodness of God and, remarkably, the Lord testified to the faith of David.

> After removing Saul, he made David their king. God testified concerning him: "I have found David son of Jesse, a man after my own heart; he will do everything I want him to do." (Acts 13:22)

***

All Things New

It was March 17, 2020. The night before, I had been overwhelmed with joy as I took a post-dinner walk around our neighborhood. I was praising the Lord for all he had done over the last several years and I was filled with hope for the future. I heard the Holy Spirit clearly say, "Behold, I am making all things new." My spirit lifted even higher at the thought.

The next morning I awakened with a splitting headache and was unable to move. I seldom get sick, so this was very unexpected. This wasn't an ordinary flu. Every cell in my body felt sick. Over my vociferous objections, my husband, Pasquale, insisted upon taking care of me. For whatever reason, he believed that he would not or could not get the virus. After approximately three days, he, too, began to feel ill. For him, however, it turned out to be much worse as it began to affect his lungs. I watched him deteriorate day after day. He became increasingly pale and weak, unable to breathe.

I prayed. I asked my friends to pray. Pasquale prayed. Nothing happened. His condition worsened. For the first time in years, I felt completely and utterly helpless. Pasquale did not want to go to the hospital. For the first time since I met him, I saw fear on his face. If he was put on a ventilator, we both knew that the odds were against him ever returning home.

Two weeks had passed and Pasquale was just a shell of his former self. I went out for a walk. Frustrated and numb, I repeatedly inquired of the Holy Spirit, "Lord, what more can I do?"

As I reached the house, I heard him say clearly, "I need you to believe."

I recalled the promise he had made me at the beginning of March, just four weeks prior—but what now seemed like an eternity away. "Lord, you told me that you are making all things new. 'All things' must include Pasquale." I entered the house, and we measured Pasquale's oxygen levels. The doctor told us to call an ambulance. It was a surreal experience, like something from a science fiction novel. The EMTs entered our house in what looked to be gas masks. On April 4, they loaded my beloved husband and ministry partner into the ambulance while our sons and I looked on.

My son asked me whether I was all right. I told him I was. I lied. All of my strength was gone. I could not pray. All I could do was remind the Lord of his promise to "make all things new." In the hospital, the doctor informed my husband that he would be put on a ventilator in the morning if his oxygen levels did not improve. All night he prayed, asking

Jesus to have mercy on me. He did not want me to suffer, so he asked the Lord to spare him.

The doctor arrived in the morning to measure his oxygen levels. He was shocked to find that they had miraculously doubled overnight. "This was not the typical progression of this virus," he declared. Pasquale explained that he had cried out to Jesus, and Jesus had answered. Five days later, he was released from the hospital and came home. To this day, our family doctor looks at him in awe. "You are a survivor," he says. "I am constantly shocked that you are even here." That is what happens when Jesus tells you he is making all things new!

***

Credible Witness

True Christian witness gives evidence for the goodness of God. It upholds his name and attests to the witness God gives about himself in Scripture, so the witness points back to God alone. The Christian witness has largely been discredited in that it has been used as a marketing tool to promote ministries and people. When Christian testimony points back to anything or any person as its focal point, it can no longer be about Christ. The apostle Paul chose not to boast of anything, but to boast only in the Lord (1 Corinthians 1:31). During his earthly ministry, Jesus desired no glory for himself but brought glory only to the Father. He didn't even want to be called "good," reserving that description exclusively for the Father. "Why do you call me good?" Jesus answered. "No one is good—except God alone" (Mark 10:18). It is unlikely he was inferring that he was not good, but rather, he was putting the inquirer's focus on God as the source of all true goodness. Jesus emptied and humbled himself, taking on a servant's nature to bring glory to the Father (Philippians 2:6-11). For the Christian witness to be truly Christian, it must first and foremost be Christlike.

A courtroom analogy easily illustrates the absurdity of testimonies being used as a marketing tool to promote ministries or people. Imagine a witness being called to testify regarding an alleged theft. Instead of answering questions pertinent to the case's facts, however, the witness

Called to Be a Witness

chooses instead to treat the courtroom as a stage. The witness then begins giving an unsolicited catalog of all their past accomplishments, wonderful qualities, and providing no evidence at all relevant to the case at hand. Such a scenario would never be tolerated in a real courtroom, but this is exactly what much of the church has done with the testimony—it has been used not to reflect the goodness of the One who is the source of the testimony, but instead as evidence for the witness.

One of the primary determinants of witness credibility or believability is the extent to which the witness could see or hear the events at issue in the case; in other words, whether the witness had firsthand knowledge of the facts to which his or her testimony pertains. If the Christian witness testifies to the goodness of God, then it presumes the witness has firsthand knowledge of God. One must experience the Lord in order to know his goodness. "Taste and see that the Lord is good" (Psalm 34:8). This demands more than intellectual knowledge; it presumes experience. The vast majority of church-going Christians have ceased to be a people of his presence by substituting religion for relationship, information for transformation, and programs for intimacy.

As believers, we are to know God and to make him known. Therefore, it follows that to make God known (to serve as a credible witness), one must know God. Once again, this requires delving into the basics of Christianity that are presumed to be self-evident, but might not be. The opportunity or invitation to "know" God is at the very heart of the new covenant.

> "This is the covenant I will make with the people of Israel after that time," declares the Lord. "I will put my law in their minds and write it on their hearts. I will be their God, and they will be my people. No longer will they teach their neighbor, or say to one another, 'Know the Lord,' because they will all know me, from the least of them to the greatest," declares the Lord. "For I will forgive their wickedness and will remember their sins no more." (Jeremiah 31:33-34)

The Giving Tree

It is a well-accepted principle that any relationship's quality is directly proportionate to the quality of the communication in that relationship. One of the primary causes of the failure of a marriage is a breakdown in communication. How is it possible, then, for anyone to claim to "know" God or to have a relationship with him in the absence of communication? Such a claim defies all logic. To know someone, by definition, means to spend time communicating with him or her. Logically speaking, therefore, to know God requires hearing from God.

Ruthven, in *What's Wrong with Protestant Theology*, asserts that if and how one hears from God is, in fact, the central issue for all humanity according to Scripture.

> Traditional human religion avoids the emphasis of Scripture which is to communicate directly and obediently with God. This experience fulfills the promise of both the Old Covenant (Ex. 20:18-19; Hebrews chapter 12), and the New Covenant which seeks to place the Spirit of God directly upon us, his prophetic words in our mouth (Isa. 59:21; Acts 2:39) and place his instructions (Jer. 31:33; 2 Cor. 3; Heb.8-12) or voice "today" (Heb. 3:7, 15; 4:7; 12:25) directly into our heart.[20]

The dichotomy is, was, and always has been between religion, which offers information "about God," and relationship, which requires an experiential knowing God. To claim to know God in the absence of actually hearing God is the equivalent of asserting knowledge of a person based solely on his or her resume. The avenue for knowing God is communicating with God, and that communication must necessarily involve hearing from him. The biblical concept of prayer is rooted in the concept of a dialogue. By definition, a dialogue is a conversation between two people in which both people have an active role in the discourse. So if only one were speaking, it would not constitute a dialogue but a monologue.

---

20. Jon Mark Ruthven, *What's Wrong with Protestant Theology: Tradition vs. Biblical Emphasis* (Tulsa, OK, Word & Spirit Press, 2013), 1.

Called to Be a Witness

In assessing the credibility of a witness, the jury will take into account the witness' personal experience and character, particularly his or her reputation for truthfulness. The voice of religion rings hollow in the ears of the unsaved who listen because it is form without substance—the appearance of God without the heart of God. At the other extreme is a Christian witness whose voice does not ring true because the actions belie the words. In certain instances, evidence of a witness' conduct outside the courtroom, which attests to his or her lack of integrity, may be introduced to discredit their testimony.

Such is the case with the witness of those who compromise obedience to the clear word of God. How can the Christian witness about a God who is holy and righteous, loving and compassionate, be believable when given by one of his "disciples" who displays none of these qualities? Can a gospel about a God *"who so loved the world that he gave his one and only Son that whoever believes in him shall not perish but have eternal life"* be believed when shared by a believer who speaks in anger, condemnation, and whose life looks no different than those who do not believe?

> The acts of the flesh are obvious: sexual immorality, impurity and debauchery; idolatry and witchcraft; hatred, discord, jealousy, fits of rage, selfish ambition, dissensions, factions and envy; drunkenness, orgies, and the like. I warn you, as I did before, that those who live like this will not inherit the kingdom of God. But the fruit of the Spirit is love, joy, peace, forbearance, kindness, goodness, faithfulness, gentleness and self-control. (Galatians 5:19-23)

In the passage above, Paul explains that those who live this way, in lawlessness, will not inherit the kingdom of God. We have to be very careful not to be so religious that we have no relationship with God, or go into lawlessness and compromise the Word of God—and lose the kingdom. Once again, the Christian witness must agree with the witness which God gives about himself. The character of a believer called to be a witness for Christ must line up with the message. Otherwise, the witness is not believable at best. At worst, the witness serves as evidence for the opposing side.

The Incalculable Cost of Silence

Testimony is highly valued, both in the courtroom and in the Bible. In both cases, the price of silence is so high that failure or refusal to testify elicits serious ramifications. In the secular courtroom, a witness can often be compelled to testify under the threat of legal sanctions. In the Bible, as in our day, the cost of silence is inestimable but rarely considered. In the Old Testament, silence (a refusal to serve as a witness for God) was never a viable option. Silence resulted in forgetting what God had done for them in the past and, therefore, who God was. When the people of Israel failed to acknowledge the truth of who God was and turned to other gods, the Lord delivered them into captivity because they had failed in their witness, thus allowing the enemies of God to blaspheme. "The men of Ephraim, though armed with bows, turned back on the day of battle; they did not keep God's covenant and refused to live by his law. They forgot what he had done, the wonders he had shown them" (Psalm 78:9-11).

Deuteronomy was the book every devout Jew had to learn by heart. This book instructed the Jewish people to remember the Lord by keeping his commandments, statutes, and the stories of God's mighty acts always on their lips and making this the foundation of their children's education. By continually meditating on and declaring God's mighty acts, the people were assured not only of never forgetting who God was, but also of passing on this knowledge to subsequent generations.

> These commandments that I give you today are to be on your hearts. Impress them on your children. Talk about them when you sit at home and when you walk along the road, when you lie down and when you get up. Tie them as symbols on your hands and bind them on your

foreheads. Write them on the doorframes of your houses
and on your gates. (Deuteronomy 6:6-9)

The first outcome of failure to witness is forgetting who God is, but it later results in his people forgetting both who they are and what they are called to do. In other words, when God's identity is lost, so is the identity of his people, as is their mission. It is, was, and always has been God's presence that determines the identity of his people and, therefore, what they can accomplish (Exodus 3:11-12; Matthew 28:20). For this very reason, there is a duty to speak—an obligation to witness—which is imposed on all who would be called by his name. The Christian witness is not optional. In fact, when asked to rebuke his disciples for giving him glory, Jesus said if they were to remain silent, the rocks would cry out (Luke 19:40). The reason for this is simple, if not self-evident. Silence begets forgetting, and in forgetting, faith erodes. Faith comes through hearing (Romans 10:17). Witness is thus a prerequisite for faith.

> How, then, can they call on the one they have not believed in? And how can they believe in the one of whom they have not heard? And how can they hear without someone preaching to them? And how can anyone preach unless they are sent? As it is written: "How beautiful are the feet of those who bring good news!" (Romans 10:14-15)

The book of Ruth is noteworthy as one of the two books in the Bible where God himself was silent, yet his presence was palpable because he was ever-present on the lips of his people. As unlikely a witness as she might have been, the embittered Naomi assured the foreigner Ruth of the goodness of God. Throughout the book of Ruth, God's blessing and his guiding hand were confirmed on his people's lips. Through their testimony, Ruth came to believe in God, held fast to him, and took her place in the bloodline of Jesus. Ruth had radical faith—the *Chutzpah* demonstrated in the parables of Jesus. That faith was birthed from hearing the praises of an extraordinary God who both provided and delivered. Apart from God, Ruth's story should have ended where it began, with a barren, impoverished widow. However, testimony birthed faith. Ruth came to know who God was and what it meant to be his child. As a result, Ruth dared to fulfill her mission and her destiny.

The lesson of Ruth holds true today. Through the Christian witness attesting to the mighty acts of God (of which the conversion experience is one), the nature and heart of God is powerfully revealed. This, in turn, reminds believers of their identity as children of God and enables them to fulfill their mission to "seek and save the lost," a mission whose success or failure is measured in terms of lives. The cost of silence in place of the Christian witness—in place of testimony to the goodness of God—is inestimable, for it is calculated in the value of countless lost souls. Silence has never been an option for a child of God, for it comes at too high a cost.

6

Sound

On Earth as it is in Heaven

All of creation carries the fingerprint of God and gives insight into the divine nature.

> Since what may be known about God is plain to them, because God has made it plain to them. For since the creation of the world God's invisible qualities—his eternal power and divine nature—have been clearly seen, being understood from what has been made, so that people are without excuse. (Romans 1:19-20)

Consequently, the operation of sound in the natural realm may provide insight into the working of sound and the word of God in the spiritual realm. Sound is of the utmost importance to God. Heaven is full of sound, the sound of praise, songs of worship, the sound of the multitudes, and the voice of God himself—the sound of "rushing waters" (Revelation 1:15). In fact, sound is absent in heaven for a span of only thirty minutes after the opening of the seventh seal (Revelation 8:1).

The book of Revelation is replete with references to sound. This is the appropriate type of "bookend" for Genesis, in which the world is birthed through sound. Thus, sound both begins and ends the Bible.

The Giving Tree

Sound is the medium of creation and the force by which everything is sustained. "The Son is the radiance of God's glory and the exact representation of his being, sustaining all things by his powerful word" (Hebrews 1:3). When God said, "let there be light" (Genesis 1:3), both sound and light were created.

Sound and light are intimately related in their origin as well as their form. Both sound and light are waves. Sound is a mechanical wave that requires a medium, such as air, liquid, or even some solids, to travel. Mechanical waves cannot travel through a vacuum. Consequently, there is no sound in space. The essence of sound is vibration, which causes the molecules of the medium to collide, creating sound waves. These waves are energy radiating from the source of the sound. Light is an electromagnetic wave that does not require a medium through which to travel. Visible light consists of different colors: red, orange, yellow, green, blue, indigo, and violet. Each hue is created by a different frequency, with red having the longest and violet having the shortest vibrational frequency. Humans are able to hear and see only approximately three percent of the overall range of sound vibration and about three percent of the entire electromagnetic spectrum.

Scientists have discovered that, at a foundational level, everything is vibrating. Not only is everything energy, but everything is also a wave with its own resonant frequency. Even physical objects are vibrating, and each object has its own resonant frequency. Human DNA, the human brain, and every organ in the human body has its own unique frequency. The heart and brain also have electromagnetic fields of energy that change depending on the person's emotional and physical state. The electromagnetic field around the heart is the most powerful field produced by the body, with over 5,000 times the brain's electromagnetic field's strength. The heart's field not only permeates every cell in the body, but it also radiates out from the body and extends into the surroundings up to ten feet away. The electromagnetic waves of one person's heart radiating out into the environment affect the brain waves of a second person standing within that range.

Sound

The earth itself is also vibrating. It emits its own resonant electromagnetic frequency called the Schumann resonance. This resonance is in the same range as the brain waves of both humans and mammals. The Schumann resonance is essential for the health and wellbeing of humans in particular. Fluctuations in the Schumann resonance have been linked to increased rates of depression, suicide, migraine headaches, and SIDS.

In the 1960's Dr. Hans Jenny proposed that everything was composed of vibrations with its own frequency. According to Jenny, the nature of the vibration determined the ultimate form of the matter. He proposed that cells with similar frequencies joined together to form an organ in the development of a human embryo. He theorized that disease resulted from disharmonious frequencies in the body. Jenny developed a machine that created three-dimensional physical images of sounds, including human vowels and tones. The pronunciation of the vowels of ancient languages such as Hebrew, Sanskrit, Egyptian, and Tibetan caused vibrations that took the shape of the written symbols for these languages. Modern languages failed to produce the same result. Jenny concluded that the sounding of sacred texts or singing the vowels from these ancient languages could transform physical reality by altering its molecular structure.

Sound is unquestionably one of the most important forces God ever created. Scientists have discovered numerous examples in nature of the power of sound waves to impact or reconfigure matter. Low-frequency sound vibrations can have a particularly powerful effect on physical matter. A pair of thirty-inch speakers connected to a tone generator can generate a note powerful enough to move a building off its foundation. In one of his experiments, inventor Nikola Tesla attached a small clock-sized electric oscillator, which emitted low-frequency vibrations, to one of the girders in a ten-story steel structure on Wall Street. The structure began to shudder within minutes, and the device had to be switched off to avoid the collapse of the entire building. Also, when a physical object's resonance is matched by a resonant frequency from outside, the effects are astonishing. For example, bridges have collapsed when the cadence of soldiers marching across it matched the resonant frequency of the bridge.

Sound or mechanical resonance has been used with great success in the field of medicine. In hospitals, kidney stones are dissolved with sound waves matching their resonant frequency. In the 1920s Dr. Royal Rife developed a machine that applied currents of specific frequencies to the human body to cure a wide range of diseases. Rife's research demonstrated that certain frequencies could cure disease while others could be used to prevent it. In 1934 the University of Southern California brought terminal cancer patients to Rife's clinic. The recovery rate of these patients was a shocking one hundred percent.

A 1992 study conducted at Eastern State University in Washington determined that the human body's average daytime frequency was between sixty-two and sixty-four hertz. A compromised immune system was associated with a drop in that frequency and created an opportunity for disease to develop. Many respected professionals believe that the source of many emotional and physical ailments and diseases are stress or trauma-induced negative energies trapped in the body's cells.

The healing properties of sound have been known for centuries. Various cultures throughout history have recognized that sound vibrations affect both human consciousness and the physical body. Historically, Chinese, Islamic, Hebrew, Egyptian, and Greek cultures have all used sound to instill cultural wisdom, heal the sick, and create altered states of consciousness. In ancient Greece, both Plato and Aristotle taught that illnesses often resulted from a disharmony in a person's state of being. The discordant state of being and thus the illness could be treated by music. Music, therefore, was the primary means of facilitating the reestablishment of a healthy resonance. The word *resonate* means a "returning, or capable of returning sound."[21] Music has also been thought to have healing properties in Christian tradition. Many famous cathedrals in Europe were acoustically designed for optimal harmonic resonance conducive to worship and prayer. The Gregorian chants were based on

---

21. Webster's Collegiate Dictionary, s.v., "resonate," (Springfield, MA: G. & C. Merriam Co, 1913).

Sound

the Solfeggio frequencies; tones believed to have transformative power and impart spiritual blessings.

***

Marc and Toby

One of my passions is to pray for children with autism, especially for their ability to communicate and connect with others. God brought me a double portion of blessing in the guise of two autistic boys, Marc and Toby. Initially, Marc and Toby were a bit shy around me. They could walk, run, and play, but neither had ever spoken a word. If ever, they rarely made eye contact and ignored my presence for the most part. Over a few weeks, they gradually began to get used to me and grew comfortable enough to sit in my lap or throw their legs over the top of mine.

I prayed for them with no visible signs of change for a few weeks. Then I heard the Holy Spirit tell me to give their mother a CD with Gregorian chants and tell her to play it when the twins were at home. Inwardly, I questioned the rationale behind this instruction. I questioned God and received no explanation, just the simple instruction. After all, the God of the universe does not have to explain himself—no matter how curious we are. Not understanding it myself, I was unable to answer the mother's questions as to why I was giving her the CD and, I provided no justification other than, "the Holy Spirit told me to give this to you."

The proof was in the pudding, as the saying goes. In a couple of weeks, the previously silent twins began to speak their first words. Was there something to the Gregorian chant, or was it simply my obedience? I may never know the answer to that question. It was enough to see God at work in the lives of Marc and Toby.

After this, the Lord sent several other children with autism for prayer. Several times, the Holy Spirit told me to sing over them, but not a typical song. He instructed me to hold a note for a while and then slowly move to the next one. I knew and still know next to nothing about autism. I was simply listening to the guidance of the Holy Spirit and trusting in his leading. It wasn't until my piano tuner came to my house when I received confirmation of what God was doing. The piano tuner was repeatedly striking the same note to make certain it was in tune before moving on to the next one.

"Neil," I said, "I love when you are all finished tuning and just play. You play so beautifully. I simply cannot stand it, though, when you keep playing the same note over and over. It grates on my nerves."

"It wouldn't grate on your nerves if you were autistic," he replied.

"What?" I asked, remembering what the Holy Spirit was telling me to do in ministry for autistic children.

"Some of the best piano tuners are autistic," he explained. "They have no issue with playing the same note repeatedly. In fact, they respond better to that than when the notes move too rapidly."

I walked away from this conversation stunned. I never checked the medical reason for this, nor did I seek any other explanation. Humbled by the whole encounter, I simply thanked God for his grace. Religion says we need more information, more knowledge, more training, and more programs. Faith, on the other hand, says God is enough.

***

The Challenge of Quantum Physics

Many assume (rather erroneously) that science and religion are at odds with each other. At the core, both science and religion are searching for the truth, albeit from differing starting points. Both science and religion frequently ask the same questions and explore much of the same territory. Prevailing scientific theories have been used throughout history to support various religious worldviews. Quantum physics, interpreted through the lens of Eastern Mysticism and as trumpeted by the New Age, has filtered through mainstream media into the contemporary mindset.

Classical physics had its origins in Isaac Newton's theories, whereby the functioning of the universe was explained through a series of mathematical formulas. According to the mathematical precision of Newtonian physics, cause and effect were certain and outcomes predictable. This age of certainty ushered in an accompanying atheistic or deistic

Sound

worldview where God was no longer a necessary piece to the universe's puzzle. In the sea of determinism, the concept of human freewill vanished as well. Classical physics and its accompanying mechanistic worldview were dominant through the beginning of the twentieth century. The basic tenets of classical physics can be summarized as follows: (1) the physical world exists independent of human observation; (2) any change in the physical universe can be explained by an analysis of the factors involved; (3) Drawing inferences from observations is a valid means for obtaining knowledge; (4) No influence of any kind can be made faster than the speed of light.

The assumed predictability of creation was shattered at the beginning of the twentieth century by discoveries emanating from the subatomic regions. Quantum theory was born when scientists discovered the atom. While touted as "new" in the mainstream media, quantum physics' theoretical and experimental bases were completed before 1930. In 1900, Max Planck discovered that radiation was emitted, not in a continuous pattern, but in packages of energy, later named "*quanta*." Therefore, at the most basic level, everything consists of small packets of energy that are constantly vibrating.

Einstein and others later determined that light was both wave-like and particle-like. Scientists have discovered that not only light, but also all subatomic particles can have both wave and particle properties, depending on the observer's expectations. The so-called "observer effect" describes that if the observer expects to see a particle, he or she will see a particle. If the observer expects to see a wave, then he or she will see a wave. In essence, then, subatomic particles seem to be able to change from particles of matter to waves of energy and back again, all according to the observer's expectations. Furthermore, in the absence of any observer, particles of light act as waves but have no precise location, existing only as "probability fields." Under observation, this probability field collapses the wave into a solid object in a specific place and time. This is referred to as "popping a qwiff."

The Giving Tree

Another quite startling discovery, often referred to as "quantum entanglement," casts doubt onto Einstein's upper limit of the speed of light. Certain experiments have demonstrated that two sub-atomic particles, which have interacted in the past, remain connected. Even after these two particles move away from each other and are separated by a great distance, they continue to behave as if they were one particle. Whatever is done to one of those particles affects the other, irrespective of the present distance between the two. This suggests that somehow information is transmitted faster than the speed of light, a physical impossibility.

Quantum physics has generated excitement in many circles, including the church. However, there remains much disagreement among scientists in the field, and the discoveries of quantum physics are, at best, incomplete. While quantum physics can give a window into the spiritual realm's possible workings, a serious note of caution is warranted. To base the validity of any worldview, Christian or otherwise, on the present state of science, quantum physics included, neglects the lessons of history and builds on shifting sand.

A Different Gospel: "Faith" and the New Age

It has taken over fifty years for quantum physics to filter into the mainstream, but philosophical and religious applications now abound. Many of the scientific theories which have filtered into mainstream thinking originated with mystical interpretations of quantum physics. Over three-and-a-half million New Agers worldwide embrace varied spiritual-philosophical interpretations of the quantum physics theories of the early to mid-twentieth centuries. In books such as Capra's *The Tao of Physics*, Wolf's *Taking the Quantum Leap*, and Zukav's *The Dancing Wu Li Masters*, theories from quantum physics have been advanced to advocate everything from monistic pantheism (the universe is an undivided whole) to positivism (people create their own reality).[22]

---

22. William Brown, "Quantum Theology: Christianity and the New Physics," *Journal of the Evangelical Theological Society*, 33/4, December 1990, 482.

Sound

Quantum physics was ushered into the mainstream for healing in 1988 with Deepak Chopra's book, *Quantum Healing*. In his book, Chopra used quantum concepts to propose a theory of psychosomatic healing. He further developed this line of reasoning in his 1993 book, *Ageless Body, Timeless Mind*, a New York Times bestseller, in which he claimed that adopting a quantum worldview could yield both healing and anti-aging results. There even was a movie released in 2004 that centered on the assertion that consciousness creates reality, an application of the observer effect, or "popping a qwiff" from quantum physics. Dr. Alan Wolf is the latest theoretical physicist to embrace a mystical interpretation. He even appeared in a movie that introduced the Law of Attraction, a concept drawn from quantum physics, according to which the observer can create material reality through intent.

Since quantum mysticism has filtered into mainstream thinking, it has also filtered into the church. Christians have unknowingly adopted many of the New Age principles, believing them to be compatible with biblical principles. The situation has become increasingly complicated by the use of Christian terminology by New Agers. From the very beginning, the cosmic battle between good and evil has always been fought in the area of truth—God's truth, to be precise. This was the serpent's strategy in the garden of Eden with his question to Eve, "Did God really say…?" The temptation of Jesus likewise centered on the truth of God. In the classic, *The Art of War* by Sun Tzu, he states that all war is based on deception and that excellence in war is achieved without fighting.[23] A war fought in the arena of truth avoids a confrontation, gaining ground not by fighting but by deception.

For over half a century, national magazines, television shows, and popular media have proclaimed the New Age. C.S. Lewis saw the battle lines clearly drawn and the final conflict between Hinduism, which absorbs all religions, and Christianity, which excludes all religions, maintaining that Jesus is the only path to God. The sad truth is that most people—both Christians and non-Christians—know very little about

---

23. Sun Tzu, *The Art of War*, translated by Lionel Giles, 1910. Public domain. Project Gutemburg accessed January 20, 2021, http://www.gutenberg.org/files/132/132-h/132-h.htm.

how evil New Age thinking really is. Ignorance is not a viable option for a Christian, and neither is compromise. In the battle over the truth, Christians must know the strategies of the enemy. Sun Tzu wrote, "If you know the enemy and know yourself, you need not fear the result of a hundred battles. If you know yourself but not the enemy, for every victory gained you will also suffer a defeat. If you know neither the enemy nor yourself, you will succumb in every battle." [24]

In the Old Testament, Moses communicated God's extreme displeasure with the inhabitants of the land of Canaan, whose practices mirrored those of the "New Age." The New Age may have a fresh title, but the practices are centuries old.

> When you enter the land the Lord your God is giving you, do not learn to imitate the detestable ways of the nations there. Let no one be found among you who sacrifices their son or daughter in the fire, who practices divination or sorcery, interprets omens, engages in witchcraft, or casts spells, or who is a medium or spiritist or who consults the dead. Anyone who does these things is detestable to the Lord; because of these same detestable practices the Lord your God will drive out those nations before you. You must be blameless before the Lord your God. (Deuteronomy 18:9-13)

The Lord has never blessed mixtures. He has always asked that his people be a holy people set apart for his glory. In new covenant terms, the people of God may be in the world but should remain apart from the world. His people must look differently, act differently, and sound differently than the world surrounding them. His sons and daughters are called to reflect the image and likeness of God himself, his DNA, as it were. Since quantum mysticism affects contemporary mindsets, one must first identify and expose the key concepts which comprise those influences. The first of these is New Age positivism. This is based on

---

24. Sun Tzu, *The Art of War*, translated by Lionel Giles, 1910. Public domain. Project Gutemburg accessed January 20, 2021, http://www.gutenberg.org/files/132/132-h/132-h.htm.

Sound

the observations in the quantum world that everything exists only in a state of potentiality, and an observer is required for that potentiality to manifest itself in reality. The most widely held view among quantum physicists is that physical objects exist only if and when they are observed. Thus, according to this view, objective reality and objective truth simply do not exist. Human beings are believed to create their own reality through their perceptions.

While it is true that quantum physics does reveal that the observer and his expectations have a significant impact on reality in the quantum field, this single concept has been appropriated by New Age teachers to suggest that each individual has the power to create his or her own reality through the power of the mind and positive affirmations. In other words, the concept that human consciousness can affect reality in the microworld has been expanded to imply that human consciousness has the potential to create reality in the macroworld as well.

The second principle from quantum mysticism which has filtered down into mainstream thinking is pantheism. The advent of quantum physics has, in effect, caused the pendulum to swing from a mechanistic world where God is no longer necessary or, at best, where he is distant and uninvolved, to one where God is everything and everything is God. This stems primarily from the superluminal transfer of information, which scientists are still grappling to understand. This phenomenon in quantum physics has been used as support for the Eastern Mystical belief of the nature and unity of all reality. According to this belief, the universe is a unified, interconnected whole. God is in all things, he is all things, and therefore, even human beings are God. It is precisely the marriage of quantum theory to Eastern Mysticism that gives credence to the New-Age worldview. The New-Age worldview is not new at all, in fact. At its core, it is nothing more than reheated pantheism served up in new packaging. It is a philosophical and theological construct in which there are no absolutes, truth is relative, and reality is subjective. It swallows up all religions for all beliefs are equal, and there any many paths to God who is impersonal, in everything, and everything. The fallacy of such logic is patently clear. In a place where everything is God,

The Giving Tree

and everyone is God, then God is nothing and no one; he is a null value without meaning because nothing is excluded.

Nevertheless, New Age "theology" with its offer of control over one's destiny through positive thoughts and intentions and positive utterance holds broad appeal to those who seek to control the circumstances of their lives and the health of their bodies. Many New Age healing modalities center around the power of the spoken word. Miracles of healing and physical health are not the only areas in which the power of positive affirmation has purported effect. Emotional wellbeing and financial prosperity are also the main areas in which people seek personal empowerment—and which the New Age promises exactly that empowerment.

A fundamental tenet of New Age is that energy follows thought. Therefore, the direction of the thoughts, positive or negative, will determine what kind of energy a person attracts. To manifest into reality, however, positive thoughts must be reinforced by positive verbal confessions. A large part of New Age practice involves the use of mantras and positive affirmations to achieve great focus and altered states of consciousness—all in an attempt to gain healing, inner transformation, and prosperity. New Agers borrow heavily from both the vocabulary and teachings of Christ. In fact, New Agers accept Jesus as a great teacher, albeit one of many, and some even invoke his name in their practices. Since all is God and all truth is relative, then all ways lead to God and Jesus is one of those ways. On the surface, this can cause great confusion. New Age seeks to achieve the outcome promised by Christ through the human will, through the flesh, and drawing on demonic power sources. They are the fruit of earthly wisdom, the Tree of the Knowledge of Good and Evil.

The Tree and the Fall of Sound

In the middle of the garden of Eden were two trees—the Tree of Life and the Tree of the Knowledge of Good and Evil. God told Adam not to eat of the Tree of Knowledge of Good and Evil, or he would surely die.

Sound

However, the third chapter of Genesis opens with a different voice, the voice of the serpent, which caused Eve to question what God had said:

> "You will not surely die," the serpent said to the woman. "For God knows that when you eat of it your eyes will be opened and you will be like God, knowing good and evil." (Genesis 3:4)

The rest of the story is history. Eve saw that the tree was pleasing to the eye and desirable for gaining wisdom, so she disobeyed God, ate, and gave some to her husband. Thus ensued the fall of mankind and the eventual expulsion from the garden. The choice presented to the first humans is the same choice that confronted Jesus in the temptation narratives. It is also the very same choice faced by every person throughout history. The Tree of the Knowledge of Good and Evil represents an attempt to gain the equivalent of divinely inspired spiritual wisdom through human effort. It seeks to procure the blessings of God, apart from God. This is the essence of spiritual formulas, which are very attractive to disenfranchised people seeking control over their lives.

Whether in the form of New Age "faith" or religion, a spiritual formula has broad appeal due to apparent mathematical precision and predictability of outcome. Not only are formulas attractive because of control, but they also offer a "guaranteed quick-fix" to many problems. Mass marketing of the contemporary New Age "wisdom" of the power of positive thinking and speaking has proved a lucrative business. Such formula-based wisdom has even filtered into the church; for example, in the excesses of the "Word of Faith" stream of the twentieth century. Due to its early excesses, particularly in financial prosperity, the Word of Faith stream has quite possibly become the most maligned stream of the independent charismatic movement. Kenneth Hagin, the father of the movement, founded the Rhema Bible Church in Broken Arrow, Oklahoma. The Word of Faith movement, however, originated with the teachings of E.W. Kenyon.

The Giving Tree

The parallels between Word of Faith theology in its most extreme form and the New Age are striking. The Word of Faith teaching asserts absolute victory for the Christian in the present. In short, it asserts that in this lifetime, Christians are entitled to all of the blessings of Abraham, including salvation, health, and financial prosperity. These blessings are, in turn, released by faith through positive confessions. It is noteworthy that Kenyon put much less emphasis on prosperity than the Word of Faith does. Moreover, he specifically recognized the difference between positive confessions in the metaphysical cults and biblical affirmations as a means of building faith. In his book, *The Hidden Man*, Kenyon delineated the difference between biblical affirmations, as he understood them, and Christian Science:

> There are two types of affirmations that I wish you to notice. First, there is the affirmation with nothing behind it but my own will to make it good. It is based on a philosophy born of sense knowledge. That sense knowledge is a product of my own mind. If it be in regard to sin, I deny the existence of it. If it be in regard to sickness, I deny the sickness has any existence. We see this in Christian Science.
>
> If it is a problem of ability to meet a financial obligation, I affirm with all of my might that I have the ability to meet it.
>
> All that I have to make these affirmations good is something that I am, or have, of myself. The Word of God has no place in this affirmation. I cannot say that greater am I than disease or greater am I than this demand upon me, consequently, my affirmation becomes a failure.
>
> The second type of affirmation is based on the Word of God.[25]

---

25. E.W. Kenyon, *The Hidden Man* (Lynnwood, WA: Kenyon's Gospel Publishing Society, Inc.) 109.

Kenyon stood against all metaphysical teachings regarding healing, including New Thought and Christian Science. He referred to such teachings as "reason darkness" and attributed their source to men's minds without the Holy Spirit.[26]

Fortunately, the Word of Faith stream has undergone some self-correction to address some of its excesses. However, the problem may be a more fundamental one. The core issue involved is what constitutes biblical faith. Nico Horn of Nambia describes "faith" in the Word of Faith movement in the following manner:

> [F]aith as a mechanism at the disposal of the believer to make him or her victorious, the belief that positive confession creates faith, and, linked with faith, changes circumstances; the belief that everyone who has faith can receive either healing from sickness or eternal health; and the belief that financial prosperity is, like healing, provided for in the atonement.[27]

If one views faith as a "mechanism at the disposal of the believer to assure his or her victory," then the resulting view of the entire Christian journey becomes one of the self-centered fulfillment of desires, wants, or needs and could not present a more conflicting view to the example of Jesus.

The Voice of Folly

The central issue in discerning counterfeit versus real spiritual power is faith. The New Age view of "faith" is one of intent. Like biblical faith, it is not a mere intellectual construct; it presses beyond the mind into the will. The word *intent* is defined as "having the mind closely directed to or bent on an object."[28] Some commentators liken Christian

---

26. Joe McIntyre, *E.W. Kenyon and His Message of Faith: The True Story* (Bothell, WA: Empowering Grace Ministries, 1997), 243.

27. Henry Lederle I, *Theology with the Spirit: The Future of the Pentecostal-Charismatic Movements in the 21st Century,* (Tulsa, OK: Word & Spirit Press, 2010), 150.

28. Webster's Collegiate Dictionary, s.v., "intent," (Springfield, MA: G. & C. Merriam Co, 1913).

faith to a kind of "intent" based on Scriptural passage such as Romans 4:17 "call(ing) into being things that were not." There is an ocean of difference between New Age faith and biblical faith. The difference lies in the origination point of the "intent," in other words, who is in control. According to the New Age, the origination point resides within the individual because they have the power and the ability to affect their circumstances, finances, health, etc., by merely thinking good thoughts and then willing those thoughts into existence through words. The sound of New Age faith is "let my will be done on earth as it is in heaven."

In contrast, biblical faith has a distinctly different sound. It is the sound of the prayer Jesus taught his disciples, "Father…your will be done on earth as it is in heaven" (Matthew 6:9-10). It is epitomized in the words of Jesus in the garden of Gethsemane, "Father…not my will but yours be done" (Luke 22:42). As defined by Ruthven in *What's Wrong with Protestant Theology*, faith is "hearing the immediate word of God and responding appropriately." It requires a submitted will. Faith requires the individual to relinquish control and simply go where God leads, do what God does, and say what he says. This is the model Jesus demonstrated during his lifetime. Behind true faith lies the deep belief in the goodness of God, which, in turn, enables surrender and obedience without calculating the cost.

The hallmark of New Age "faith" is the belief that the speaker can use positive thoughts expressed as positive verbal confessions to alter their circumstances to gain material benefits, health, or emotional well-being. The key to New Age thinking lies in the power to manipulate and control. On the other hand, Christians make a tragic error when they enter into such thinking, believing that they have the right to demand or claim their inheritance. It's just like when the prodigal son demanded his inheritance from his father. In contrast, the example of Jesus is one of humility. Jesus is, after all, the example to be followed. Jesus approached the Father as a son, but with humility. He knew that only grace allows us to even approach God at all.

Sound

Once again this all turns on the biblical definition of faith: "to hear God and respond appropriately." Biblical faith at its heart requires an intimate relationship with God as Father, but also allows him to remain God. The book of Job, a startling account of the unfathomable divide between the human and divine understanding of justice, fits nowhere into the theology of faith as a tool for the assurance of the individual's victory during this lifetime. Job, a righteous man who had enjoyed intimate friendship and blessings from God, was severely tested by the loss of his children, wealth, and health. Job, whose admirable initial response was worship, was later admonished by God for his utter lack of understanding.

The Lord said to Job:

> "Will the one who contends with the Almighty correct him? Let him who accuses God answer him!" Then Job answered the Lord: "I am unworthy—how can I reply to you? I put my hand over my mouth. I spoke once, but I have no answer—twice, but I will say no more." Then the Lord spoke to Job out of the storm: "Brace yourself like a man; I will question you, and you shall answer me. "Would you discredit my justice? Would you condemn me to justify yourself? Do you have an arm like God's, and can your voice thunder like his? Then adorn yourself with glory and splendor, and clothe yourself in honor and majesty. (Job 40:2-10)

The desire "to be like God," as so aptly phrased by the crafty serpent of Genesis, is at the root of the Tree of the Knowledge of Good and Evil. To eat of that tree implies the point of origin is one of pride, of elevating oneself to the position of God, of being in control of outcomes, of circumstances, and, at the extreme, of other people. Pride is the root for wanting to control others, which then develops into witchcraft. It may not start out as occult practice, but the work of the flesh—if left unchecked—will eventually lead to the occult. Whenever anyone seeks to procure spiritual power to reengineer their own reality or that of someone else according to their will, that is the very definition of witchcraft.

While the New Age touts the power of positive confession, there is also a control element inherent in negative confession. New Age "faith" is, at its core, about control and confessing the individual's will into circumstances. On the other hand, God never manipulates or controls people, nor does he authorize the use of words or his power to manipulate or control others. Jesus is called the Word, and believers should, therefore, be vigilant as to the words they speak.

The misuse of words by believers comes in two areas. The first area is the words Christians speak about one another. The second is the words they speak to God in prayer. In the New Testament, Paul instructs Christians to "slander no one," which includes believers and nonbelievers alike (Titus 3:2). The word translated as "slander" is *blasphemo*, from which the word *blaspheme* is derived. It is important to recognize that the sin of blasphemy applies to evil words spoken against God and words spoken against human beings, who are made in the image of God. The epistle of James deals more specifically with words spoken against fellow believers: "Brothers and sisters, do not slander one another" (James 4:11). The legal term *slander* excludes any statement which is true, and that is how many Christians interpret its meaning. The Greek word translated as "slander" is *katalalo,* which merely means to "speak against" and has no such connotation that the statement be false. Consequently, believers are admonished not to speak badly of fellow believers, even if what is said is true.

In fact, gossip and slander originate in a desire to control others. Most Christians view gossip and slander as relatively harmless, but Scripture contains dire warnings about the misuse of words and the power of the tongue. Jesus himself said that everyone must account for every empty or idle word spoken.

> But I tell you that everyone will have to give account
> on the day of judgment for every empty word they have

spoken. For by your words you will be acquitted, and by your words you will be condemned. (Matthew 12:36-37).

Gossip and slander are fruit of the Tree of the Knowledge of Good and Evil because they are judgments made against another person based on human insight and wisdom apart from God. These negative words are disobedience of the worst sort and echo the sound of the devil, whose name means "slanderer" and whose role is the accuser of the brethren. Words spoken against a person tear down the value of the soul and God's image in that individual. According to Jesus in the Sermon on the Mount, this is equivalent to murder and puts the speaker in danger of the fire of hell (Matthew 5:21-22).

The inherent dangers of gossip and slander are made apparent by the descending order of the adjectives used by James in his epistle. What begins as earthly and of the flesh eventually descends into the realm of the demonic.

> Out of the same mouth come praise and cursing. My brothers and sisters, this should not be. Can both fresh water and salt water flow from the same spring? My brothers and sisters, can a fig tree bear olives, or a grapevine bear figs? Neither can a salt spring produce fresh water. Who is wise and understanding among you? Let them show it by their good life, by deeds done in the humility that comes from wisdom. But if you harbor bitter envy and selfish ambition in your hearts, do not boast about it or deny the truth. Such "wisdom" does not come down from heaven but is earthly, unspiritual, demonic. (James 3:10-15)

Words spoken in gossip and slander are not normally viewed by Christians as curses, but Scripture says otherwise. The effect is the same. Negative words about fellow Christians are channels through which demonic power is released against members of the body of Christ. The believer who is guilty of these kinds of words defiles themselves along with other believers (James 3:6).

The second area in which believers misuse their words (and in which the potential for harm is even greater) is in prayers uttered to God. Prayer to God must never be an avenue to either accuse a fellow believer or seek to control a person. At the root of such prayers is a desire to manipulate or control, in fact, "playing God" in someone else's life. Any prayer that seeks to override God's sovereignty in a believer's life is not from the Holy Spirit but is based on counterfeit spiritual authority. Any time someone is manipulating and controlling others, they are using witchcraft, because this type of behavior doesn't come through the Holy Spirit.

No one has the right or the authority to pray his or her will into someone else's life. No prayer is powerless. The question then becomes whether the effect of the prayer for a person will be positive or negative. Prayers motivated by wrong heart attitudes are not empowered by the Holy Spirit but are soulish, counterfeit, and release demonic power. Meanwhile, Holy Spirit-led prayers are based on true spiritual authority and have the most beautiful and life-changing results.

7

Grace Notes from Heaven

Let there be Light

It is impossible to discuss the sound of God without discussing the heart of God, for his sound emanates from his heart. To endeavor to speak on behalf of God unmotivated by the heart of God is form without substance and brings him no honor. God's sound originates from his heart, from the very core of his being. That center is love, for God is love (1 John 4:8). Religion, the god of the Pharisees of Jesus' time, is alive and well today and offers a distant and angry god whose wrath cannot be appeased and whose approval must be earned. This god remains aloof, disconnected from and disinterested in the affairs of the men and women he created. This god of religion bears no resemblance whatsoever to the God of the Bible—the God of Abraham, Isaac, and Jacob, the God who declares, "The Lord your God is with you, the Mighty Warrior who saves. He will take great delight in you; in his love he will no longer rebuke you, but will rejoice over you with singing" (Zephaniah 3:17). The God of heaven sings? In fact, to the ears of religion, this is unfathomable. But it is biblical truth. Not only does God sing, he also rejoices over his sons and daughters in song.

Many people struggle to find the loving God of the New Testament in the pages of the Old. The Bible, in fact, is held together by one single unifying theme: God's love manifested through grace. God's grace is everywhere, always beckoning, always drawing back into the Father's heart. God's sound is infused with this grace. The Hebrew word for *sound* is *Qol,* which means "sound, noise, or voice." The first mention of God's sound in Scripture immediately followed the sin of Adam and Eve when they listened to another sound in the garden, the voice of the serpent. After they ate the forbidden fruit, Adam and Eve heard the *sound* of the Lord walking in the garden. God went looking for them. He called out to them, inquiring where they were (Genesis 3:8-9). The sound of God, the call of God to Adam and Eve, resonated throughout all of creation. All was not lost. Redemption was on the way. Adam and Eve heard the sound of God's footsteps followed by the sound of his voice. They heard the sound of God's redemption, which would ultimately find its completion in the finished work of the cross, in the Word of God Incarnate. God's sound is redemptive, beckoning, inviting, urging to come back home into the Father's house.

The sound of God not only reflects his heart but it carries his nature, the essence of who he is. God is the Creator of the universe. His sound, his voice, his word, therefore, is creative. God's voice doesn't just *sound like* something. It *does* something. God's sound creates out of nothing, brings order to chaos, creates hope and a future, gives life to the driest of bones, and raises the dead. The opening chapters of Genesis portrayed a picture of utter hopelessness—the earth was formless and empty, and darkness covered the surface of the deep. Suddenly, the picture shifted. The Spirit of God hovered over the water and declared, "Let there be light." Sound from the mouth of God instantly brought hope—"there was light." God has not changed, and neither has the power of his word to accomplish what it is released to do.

> So is my word that goes out from my mouth: It will not return to me empty, but will accomplish what I desire and achieve the purpose for which I sent it. (Isaiah 55:11)

God released his sound and disorder became beauty. God spoke and darkness became light. The pattern of creation has never changed.

Grace Notes from Heaven

It is vitally important to note not only what God's sound is but also what it is not. God did not look at the situation in Genesis and say, "What a mess!" He didn't focus on the darkness or the disarray. Instead, he saw vision, possibility, and destiny. Then he spoke what he saw into being. As mentioned earlier, light and sound are related. Just as light can be seen and sound heard, so are hearing and sight related. Faith comes from hearing the word of God (Romans 10:17), but it facilitates vision. In other words, hearing produces faith, but faith produces sight. Hearing and sight in God's kingdom are inextricably linked. Faith has often been juxtaposed with sight. Ironically, one of the judgments leveled at the followers of Jesus is that faith is most certainly blind. Indeed, Paul taught the Corinthians to "live by faith, not by sight" (2 Corinthians 5:7). However, the conclusion that faith—hearing the immediate word of God and responding appropriately— is opposed to sight, is both unfounded and unbiblical. Faith is in opposition only to human sight, fleshly discernment, and limited earthly perspective. Faith originates with hearing the word of God and actually creates sight—sight from heaven's perspective.

> I keep asking that the God of our Lord Jesus Christ, the glorious Father, may give you the Spirit of wisdom and revelation, so that you may know him better. I pray that the eyes of your heart may be enlightened in order that you may know the hope to which he has called you, the riches of his glorious inheritance in his holy people, and his incomparably great power for us who believe. (Ephesians 1:17-19)

God has not changed. He is still in the business of the miraculous. He still brings order to the chaos, light to the darkness, and life to the barren places. God is still the Creator, and he is still in the creation business.

***

The Giving Tree

Stephanie

Stephanie, a woman in her early twenties, approached the altar for prayer. She had cystic fibrosis, a genetic disease about which I knew next to nothing. Listening for the guidance of the Holy Spirit, I heard these words, "Rearrange the genes."

"What?" I was incredulous. Surely, he couldn't be serious. "I am going to look like a fool," I thought to myself. "Everyone is watching me." Then, another thought crowded the previous concern for my reputation from my mind. "God created her genes, so certainly he can rearrange them." Then I slowly and quietly said, "In the name of Jesus, I command this woman's genes to be rearranged for perfect health." Stephanie stared at me in disbelief. I relayed to her the thought that was in my mind, "Is God not the Creator of all, including your genes?" She smiled and nodded in agreement. It was impossible to ascertain at that moment whether Stephanie had been healed.

Approximately eight years later, I was attending a meeting at my son's school when an unfamiliar woman approached me, insisting that I had prayed for her daughter. In tears, she presented me with a picture of a healthy, happy, and more mature Stephanie surrounded by her loving family, which now consisted of a husband and two children. According to the doctors, Stephanie would not live past puberty. The odds of her survival were dismal, but her mother had not given up hope and God had a plan. He who had created Stephanie would see her through, not only to adulthood, but also to becoming a mother herself by "simply" rearranging her genes.

***

Hearing and Seeing as a Child of God

There is an order in the kingdom of God and an order to seeing as God sees. First, hearing enables one to know God better or to see God as he is. God's sound releases faith to see that God is love, and the false image of God shatters. Second, God's sound affects the hearer's identity. Hearing the voice of God not only topples the false god of religion, but it also shatters the false image of self. To see oneself from God's viewpoint is to see oneself as a beloved son or daughter. Third, the sound of

God enables one to see others as God sees them—as beloved children of God. Hearing God facilitates knowing God is love: I am loved, and others are equally loved by God. Fourth, hearing God gives vision or destiny. It opens up heaven's perspective "to know the hope to which he has called you, the riches of his glorious inheritance in his holy people, and the incomparably great power for us who believe."

Moses was tending his father-in-law's sheep on Mount Horeb when he saw a burning bush and heard the voice of God. Moses' initial reaction was resistance to his destiny, continually doubting despite numerous assurances from God. The text reveals the Hebrew verb *ra'ah* "to see" is used many times about both Moses attempting "to see" and of God's ability "to see." The word *ra'ah* not only means "to see" but also "to understand." In this passage, Moses clearly had no sight, no vision, and no understanding of who God was, of who he himself was, or of God's ability to bring forth the destiny of his people. At this point in his life, Moses was in desperate need of heaven's perspective, of faith, and of the sight produced by faith.

When God saw Moses, he saw his destiny. "Since then, no prophet has risen in Israel like Moses, whom the Lord knew face to face" (Deuteronomy 34:10). Every human being is created for a purpose. Faith has the vision to discern that purpose. As with Moses, God did not focus on the clumsiness, on the obstacles, on Moses' failures and shortcomings. God saw who Moses would become. God saw destiny, then he spoke it into existence. God's sound, even when corrective, is redemptive. Negative correction can never originate in the heart of God because it is at odds with it. The sound of God gives vision, a possibility for his son or daughter to live into, facilitating a confrontation with any spiritual bondage and sin in a redemptive manner. A word from God establishes identity and, in doing so, separates that which is in opposition to that identity.

The mission of Jesus is redemptive, and his redemption is never partial but always complete. Every believer in Christ has experienced at least one miracle, and that miracle is salvation. Salvation is the beginning of

The Giving Tree

redemption by healing the chasm between man and God created by sin. God's redemption in Christ Jesus encompasses the whole of creation and the whole of every believer. Once separation between the believer and God is healed, redemption can then begin within the soul. The soul consists of the mind, will, and emotions, and, as noted above, his or her very life. The regeneration of a person's spirit, which comes with salvation, enables direct communication and communion with God.

> Yet to all who did receive him, to those who believed in his name, he gave the right to become children of God. (John 1:12)

The right to become a child of God becomes a reality with a life lived as a child of God—a life lived by faith—"hearing God and responding appropriately." This is the key to the abundant life Jesus promised and the very reason for which he came. The regeneration which took place in the spirit must happen in the soul as well. The finished work of the cross of Christ included a redeemed soul—a renewed mind, healed emotions, and a redeemed imagination. The mind controls intellectual capacities and information processing; emotions are governed by the conscience and dictate how a person relates to other people. The will contains our desires as well as the creative capacities of the soul.

One word from God can change everything. Ironically, Jesus, whose name is the Word, was a man of very few words. Every word he spoke had a purpose and accomplished what it was sent to do. In his estimation, lengthy prayers were not only unnecessary but also undesirable. Such wisdom flies in the face of contemporary logic where more is better, lengthy prayers reflect righteousness, and form precedes substance. In contrast, Jesus used his words sparingly, imbuing each one with tremendous worth and power. Contemporary believers should be as careful and discerning with their words.

> For the word of God is alive and active. Sharper than any double-edged sword, it penetrates even to dividing soul

and spirit, joints and marrow; it judges the thoughts and attitudes of the heart. (Hebrews 4:12)

***

One Word

One word from the Lord can change everything. A few years ago, I received an invitation to speak in New Jersey at a Korean women's group. The requested topic was deliverance, and the audience was only partly English-speaking, so I would have to work through a translator. I knew the situation would be a bit complex, but I agreed nonetheless.

I arrived to find a group of eight to ten women already seated around an oblong table. The pastor sat to my left and agreed to do the translating. As I began to teach my well-planned lesson, I felt the Holy Spirit tell me that this was not what he wanted. I started a silent internal dialogue, the existence of which was known only to the Holy Spirit and me. "Lord," I objected, "these people asked me here so I could teach on deliverance, and that is what I agreed to do. I can't just start teaching something else."

At this point, the pastor stopped me and said, "Sherri, it's okay. Just teach what the Lord is telling you to teach. It doesn't have to be deliverance."

I felt the Lord telling me to share my testimony of abuse in my former marriage. As I began to open up the details of my former life and God's healing, silent tears started to flow down the women's cheeks around the table. The Holy Spirit kept whispering a word I didn't want to share in a cultural context I did not completely understand. A word I knew had serious issues with shame. That word was *abortion*. Finally, I turned to the pastor and whispered the word I kept hearing. She translated it to the group. One woman fell to the floor sobbing and muttering something in Korean that I could not understand.

Attempting to understand what was happening and what God could possibly want me to do in this situation, I requested that the pastor translate. The pastor explained that the woman's husband had an extramarital affair, and the mistress became pregnant and had an abortion. This woman, his wife, had found out about it and was devastated.

The Giving Tree

The words she kept repeating to herself in Korean were: "It is okay that he doesn't love me." The pastor and I ministered to her together. She was in desperate need of inner healing and the knowledge that she was lovable and was deserving of love. This was just the beginning of a group healing session during which every woman in the group, without exception, shared the details of her personal pain in her relationships and received inner healing from the Lord. All of this was the result of one word from the Lord.

***

God's sound, his word, separates the true from the false in one's identity. It penetrates to the deepest portions of the soul, releases potential, and deposits a seed of destiny. A word from God breathes life into a broken soul and resurrects a dead spirit. Physical and emotional healing can often result from one well-timed word from God.

> The hand of the Lord was on me, and he brought me out by the Spirit of the Lord and set me in the middle of a valley; it was full of bones. He led me back and forth among them, and I saw a great many bones on the floor of the valley, bones that were very dry. He asked me, "Son of man, can these bones live?" I said, "Sovereign Lord, you alone know." Then he said to me, "Prophesy to these bones and say to them, 'Dry bones, hear the word of the Lord! This is what the Sovereign Lord says to these bones: I will make breath enter you, and you will come to life. I will attach tendons to you and make flesh come upon you and cover you with skin; I will put breath in you, and you will come to life. Then you will know that I am the Lord.'" (Ezekiel 37:1-6)

The story of the Samaritan woman at the well is illustrative in this respect. Quite intentionally, Jesus "had" to go through Samaria to meet with the woman at the well. This meeting took place near Shechem, the very place where Joshua gathered the people to pronounce the blessings and curses of the Mosaic Covenant, with half of the nation standing in front of Mount Gerizim to pronounce the blessings for obedience, and half of the nation in front of Mount Ebal to pronounce the curses which would result from disobedience (Joshua 8:33). The people in Shechem later confirmed this covenant. Not only did the people act as witnesses on behalf of their choice to serve the Lord, but they set up a stone as a witness should they break their word (Joshua 24:21-27). It is in this very place—between the curses and the blessings—that God's sound changed the Samaritan woman's life forever.

The Samaritan woman encountered the Living Word of God at the well. Yet, where are the signs, wonders, miracles, and fanfare associated with the sound of God? The greatest miracles often come with little fanfare. The sound of God often is not a trumpet but a whisper discerned only in stillness.

> Then a great and powerful wind tore the mountains apart and shattered the rocks before the Lord, but the Lord was not in the wind. After the wind there was an earthquake, but the Lord was not in the earthquake. After the earthquake came a fire, but the Lord was not in the fire. And after the fire came a gentle whisper. When Elijah heard it, he pulled his cloak over his face and went out and stood at the mouth of the cave. (1 Kings 19:11-13)

Identity Shift

The meeting between Jesus and the Samaritan woman at the well arguably resulted in one of the greatest of Jesus' miracles. No blind eyes were opened, nor did the lame walk, a child's lunch did not multiply to feed thousands, and the demonic realm did not flee in terror at the approach of Jesus. Nevertheless, a miracle happened, a miracle of epic proportions. The Word of God did not return empty, but accomplished that very purpose for which he "had" to go through Samaria. Jesus came "to seek and save what was lost" (Luke 19:10), and so he did. God's priorities in releasing his sound are rooted in his heart. Often the expectation is that God's sound revolves around action and around doing something. God's sound, however, brings order, and the top priority tends to be identity. Apart from identity, there can be no consequent action, at least action which bears lasting fruit. It is this shift in identity which lies at the very core of the new covenant. "Yet to all who did receive him, to those who believed in his name, he gave the right to become children of God— children born not of natural descent, nor of human decision or a husband's will, but born of God" (John 1:12-13).

In other words, the mission of Jesus, the Word of God, was to grant each person the right to become a child of God. The story of the Samaritan woman at the well clearly outlines God's priorities in releasing his sound. God is first and foremost in the communication business to restore lost identity. In other words, God often speaks to do a miracle inside a person before he speaks to do something for or with that person. The greatest realization someone can have is that they are a son or daughter of God. One word from God can change a life!

"And I tell you that you are Peter, and on this rock I will build my church, and the gates of Hades will not overcome it" (Matthew 16:18). First things must remain first. Identity must come before mission. Simply put, the mission to "be fruitful and multiply" or to "make disciples" implies replicating one's DNA. That DNA must, in turn, reflect the DNA of God. According to the teaching Jesus delivered to the Samaritan woman, God seeks worshipers who will worship him in spirit and in truth. He seeks children after his own heart. To reproduce spiritual children for God, the individual must first understand that he or she is a child of God. Broken souls damaged by rejection and the cruelty of this world and even by the church desperately need the living water Jesus offered to the woman at the well. That living water is the sound of a God who loves without condition, forgives without remembering, saves without qualification, and whose power to redeem knows no limits. This is the sound of God's heart and it is the essence of his word. The greatest miracles are from the inside out. They are miracles of the heart. The answer to the struggle of what it means to be a child of God is God's sound.

Jesus was perfectly and acutely aware of the state of the Samaritan's woman's life, just as he was with the woman caught in adultery, as well as the sinful woman who anointed his feet—and all of the other sinners he befriended. Not once in any of these scenarios did Jesus accuse, condemn, or berate these people for their failures. It is always the desire of God to redeem, to seek and save the lost. Broken people need restoration. Oppressed people need freedom. The poor and disenfranchised need a voice, a choice, and value. The sound of God reflects the heart of God and the perspective of heaven. It isn't that sin is acceptable; it most certainly is not. God simply knows that he is enough; that love is enough. Love heals, love restores, and in fact, always accomplishes its goal. Quite simply, love never fails.

The majority of people believe "holiness" connotes sinless perfection. Consequently, its opposite would be "sinful." The true meaning of *holiness* is to be "set apart." Therefore, its true opposite is "common." Jesus said his disciples would be distinguished or set apart by their love for one another. The love displayed in his disciples' lives would not be common, but would set them apart, making them shine like stars in a wicked and perverse generation (see Philippians 2:15). This is what it means to be conformed into the image of Christ.

The Lamb Who Roared

> In the beginning was the Word, and the Word was with God, and the Word was God. He was with God in the beginning. Through him all things were made; without him nothing was made that has been made. (John 1:1-3)

The gospel of John opens with one of the most ringing affirmations of the divinity of Jesus Christ. This passage states unequivocally that he is God, and it calls him the Word, who was from the beginning. Everything without exception was made through this Word, and only through the Word of Jesus can life be found. Jesus himself told his disciples that his words were "Spirit and life" (John 6:63). During his earthly ministry,

The Giving Tree

Jesus demonstrated the kingdom of God in both word and deed. The words he spoke were imbued with life—they had power. In fact, while Jesus sometimes healed through touch, the method he used most often was the spoken word. It was the exclusive method used for driving out demons: "He drove out the spirits with a word" (Matthew 8:16).

Nowhere in any of the gospel accounts do the words of Jesus ever fail to accomplish the end for which they were spoken. In short, they had the power to transform the reality of physical circumstances, among other things, to bring salvation, healing, wholeness, and freedom. Jesus demonstrated what it means to release God's sound. Jesus uttered the very words of God, and those words, in turn, released the kingdom of God.

Throughout history, God has used people to carry his sound throughout the earth. He has raised up voices whose primary task was to turn God's people back to him by reminding them of the miraculous things he had done.

> After that whole generation had been gathered to their ancestors, another generation grew up who knew neither the Lord nor what he had done for Israel. (Judges 2:10)

God's mighty acts told the story of who God was and who they were as a people chosen by God. Jesus, the Word, was the ultimate voice in this sense, serving as a living testimony to the heart of the Father. Jesus said, "Anyone who has seen me, has seen the Father" (John 14:9).

It is a common but erroneous assumption that Jesus performed miracles because he was God. Quite to the contrary, Jesus never used the power from his divinity while on earth. Instead, Jesus performed miracles as a man anointed by the Holy Spirit.

> How God anointed Jesus of Nazareth with the Holy Spirit and power, and how he went around doing good

and healing all who were under the power of the devil,
because God was with him. (Acts 10:38)

This is the same basis on which believers today are called to continue the ministry of Jesus.

But you will receive power when the Holy Spirit comes
on you; and you will be my witnesses in Jerusalem, and
in all Judea and Samaria, and to the ends of the earth.
(Acts 1:8)

The duty of God's witnesses is to be a voice—his voice—to remind people of what God has done and to give hope for what God is going to do. This creates an environment where people can come to know God through his mighty acts. The miracles of God, in turn, reveal the heart of God. As was particularly evident in the ministry of Jesus, God uses his power to demonstrate his love. When sickness is healed, when a soul is restored, when freedom is granted to the oppressed, this is all visible and tangible evidence of the love of God. This is the kingdom of God crashing into the here and now—a reign and rule that reflects the heart of a loving Father. Throughout Scripture, God displays an inordinate concern for those in difficult circumstances, like the poor, the orphan, and the widow. God delights in wielding his power on behalf of the powerless.

God created everything from the sound of his powerful word, speaking into existence all that is in both the seen and unseen realms. The power of the spoken word to change reality defies the logic and rationality of the world. Even more astonishing is that God would choose to share the responsibility for creation with humankind. God entrusted Adam with the naming of the animals. Before the day sound fell, Adam was involved in the creative process together with God as one who heard the voice of God, saw what God saw, and said what God said. This was a divine partnership in the creative process ordained by God.

The Giving Tree

The day Adam and Eve chose to eat from the Tree of the Knowledge of Good and Evil was the day that sound fell. The intimate relationship and seamless communication which once existed as Adam and Eve walked and talked with God in the garden were broken by sin. Jesus, the Word, came to redeem that communication, that relationship, and the entirety of sound. He was intimately connected to the Father, heard what he said, saw what he saw, and said what he said. He did all of this as a man empowered by the Holy Spirit, thus leaving his disciples with a legacy and an example to follow. Even Jesus, who is God in the flesh, would not judge by what he heard, nor decide by what he saw, but would rely on the Holy Spirit, the source of wisdom from God.

> A shoot will come up from the stump of Jesse; from his roots a Branch will bear fruit. The Spirit of the Lord will rest on him—the Spirit of wisdom and of understanding, the Spirit of counsel and of might, the Spirit of the knowledge and fear of the Lord—and he will delight in the fear of the Lord. He will not judge by what he sees with his eyes, or decide by what he hears with his ears; but with righteousness he will judge the needy, with justice he will give decisions for the poor of the earth. (Isaiah 11:1-4)

Humility: The Keynote of Heaven

Throughout history, an inordinate amount of attention has been devoted to the theologies of man, to "big names," and to pomp and circumstance. The unfortunate result is a comparison and a plumbline which are unbiblical. Scripture sets Jesus alone as perfect theology. There is no other standard by which to measure other than Jesus Christ. Jesus is the Alpha and the Omega, beginning and the end, the way, and everything in between. In Jesus, everything holds together. He sustains everything in all of creation (Hebrews 1:3), and in him, all things hold together (Colossians. 1:17).

Grace Notes from Heaven

The book of Revelation declares the servants of God to be those "who hold to the testimony of Jesus." Furthermore, "the testimony of Jesus is the spirit of prophecy" (Revelation 19:10 ESV). The statement contains within itself a mathematical simplicity. The two sides of the equation "testimony of Jesus" and the "spirit of prophecy" are equivalent. Perhaps, as is the case with the concept of "faith," the first part of the equation seems so basic, almost too simple, to warrant theologians' attention. However, since the statement is one of equivalency, logically, the second half of the statement—prophecy—cannot and should not be evaluated except in light of the first part. Thus, at the foundational level lies the question of what constitutes the testimony of Jesus. The testimony of Jesus is the spirit that motivates speaking the words of God.

As mentioned in chapter 4, "testimony" is the verbal evidence given by a witness. It is a legal or courtroom term, and it is from that context its biblical usage is derived. Therefore, it is the verbal eyewitness accounts (later recorded in written form in Scripture) from people with firsthand knowledge of the words, actions, and miracles of Jesus which constitute the testimony of Jesus. These words and deeds attest to the truth of who he is. They make up the "case for Christ."

This is a time when many have become so enamored with the size of ministries and the influence of man that they have lost sight of what is really important. The cross of Christ and the mission it symbolizes is the enduring centerpiece of the word of God. It was the reason for which Jesus came; a plan laid out from the foundation of the world. "The Lamb who was slain from the creation of the world" (Revelation 13:8). The mystery of the cross was revealed to the prophets (see Acts 4:11). All of their voices in unison spoke about it, predicted it, and looked forward to it. Any sound out of harmony with the message of the cross will ultimately be out of tune with the heart of God. The cross goes against the grain of everything that Western culture holds dear, of everything valued and prized by man. It reflects values that fly in the face of pride, power, possessions, and prestige. It contradicts the messages of self-exultation and the pursuit of self-fulfillment. The cross symbolizes a kingdom not of this world, but a kingdom where the way up is down, foolish things shame the wise, and where power is perfected in weakness.

Above all else, the cross is ultimately a symbol of humility. The cross declares that God, who is omnipotent, omniscient, and all-sufficient, is also completely humble. This is the very reason the cross should shock the senses. The cross is nonsense when viewed from the vantage point of human wisdom. It is wisdom gained through a heart that is connected with God. The humility of the cross is the single factor that differentiates Christianity from every other religion. Humility is not only the very heart of the Christian faith, but it is also the most important prerequisite for discipleship. The testimony of Jesus is first and foremost the story of a humble God who came down to do for his creatures what they could not do for themselves:

> Who, being in very nature God, did not consider equality with God something to be used to his own advantage; rather, he made himself nothing by taking the very nature of a servant, being made in human likeness. And being found in appearance as a man, he humbled himself by becoming obedient to death—even death on a cross! (Philippians 2:5-8)

From a wooden manger to a wooden cross, humility is the single defining characteristic in the life of Jesus Christ. Jesus is at the same time the Good Shepherd and the Lamb who was slain. Humility is the very root of the Tree of Life. It is the heart attitude of heaven. It is the sound that declares, "God is enough." Humility is the sound of the Holy Spirit who spoke through David in Psalm 23. It is the sound of the voices of the prophets who looked forward to the time of Jesus. It is the sound from the Father's heart echoed in the voices of the present-day disciple. Humility is the disposition of the soul that enables trust. It is a heart attitude, resulting in the proper estimation of both God and self. Simply stated, humility allows God to be God.

Humility is the very reason God's kingdom defies all human logic. It is the sound of heaven where "power is made perfect in weakness" (2 Corinthians 12:9), and "the least is the greatest" (Luke 9:48). God takes great joy in using the unlikely, the despised, and the lowly to do great things for him, precisely because it magnifies him. He alone is God and will share his glory with no other. Based on this, heaven will certainly contain some surprises. Humankind tends to measure "success" by the wrong standards. According to heaven, victory is found on the lowest ground, power is perfected in weakness, and wisdom is given to the childlike. In the kingdom of God, victory is found in precisely the place where earth would declare defeat. True victory is found in the place where the Lion appears as the Lamb.

> "See, the Lion of the tribe of Judah, the Root of David, has triumphed. He is able to open the scroll and its seven seals." Then I saw a Lamb, looking as if it had been slain, standing at the center of the throne. (Revelation 5:5-6)

Humility is not one virtue among many. It is the nexus and the attribute which holds all of the other virtues in place. It is the root of the tree without which the tree itself cannot exist. Humility is the attitude of the heart that enables complete dependence on and trust in God. As such, one can have no more faith than he or she has of humility. If faith is "to hear God and respond appropriately," then faith is possible only to the extent there is trust. Jesus is the Word through whom all of creation has its origins and existence. To him belongs all authority, all honor, and all power, yet he laid it all down and became like a sheep entirely dependent on his Father. Jesus set an example of complete dependence on the Father. "Very truly I tell you, the Son can do nothing by himself; he can do only what he sees his Father doing, because whatever the Father does the Son also does" (John 5:19). Jesus lived his life in complete dependence on his Father, doing only what he saw his Father doing, and speaking only the words of the Father.

The Giving Tree

> Don't you believe that I am in the Father, and that the Father is in me? The words I say to you I do not speak on my own authority. Rather, it is the Father, living in me, who is doing his work. (John 14:10)

Trust in God means relying on God as a promise-keeper and on his faithfulness to his word. Rather ironically, Jesus, the Word and the Bread of Life, is the very picture of what it means to live not by bread alone but by every word which proceeds out of the mouth of God (Deuteronomy 8:3). Humility is truly the root of the Tree of Life. Everything else grows up from this root and reflects its nature. Therefore, humility should be the most admired and sought-after characteristic of Christ. Everything is upside down in God's kingdom; the least are the greatest, and the humble are the most powerful.

Humility brings freedom and releases destiny, for humility does away with all yokes of human origin, yokes of unrealistic expectations, and human standards of measurement and success. Rest can be found only in humility, in the heart attitude that finds identity as a beloved child of God. Only this heart attitude trusts enough to allow God the freedom to be God. Humility enables trust in the faithfulness of God. Then all striving ceases. The yoke of Jesus is light.

> Come to me, all you who are weary and burdened, and I will give you rest. Take my yoke upon you and learn from me, for I am gentle and humble in heart, and you will find rest for your souls. For my yoke is easy and my burden is light. (Matthew 11:28-30)

It is in this place of dependence on God and trust in his faithfulness that the child of God becomes truly free to walk in his or her unique destiny and to add his or her voice to the harmony of heaven.

> In 2007, Harvard Medical School and MIT conducted research on the sound obtained from the DNA taken from human blood samples. Since the formula for DNA

can be converted to a logical alphanumeric sequence, it can be transformed into musical notes. Research fellow Gil Alterovitz at M.I.T. and Harvard Medical School have developed a computer program that translates the raw material from DNA into specific musical notes. Since every person has a unique DNA, each person has a unique song; in fact, in every case, the DNA sequence produced a melody.[29]

Listen for the Fruit

One can only have as much faith as he or she has humility. The same is true of love. The capacity for love is predicated on a heart attitude of humility. In other words, humility enables love while pride makes it impossible.

In the Catholic church, there is a process by which certain marriages can be declared "null" or, in other words, so lacking from the outset of an essential element that the relationship never constituted a "true marriage." A detailed analysis is beyond the present scope, but one basis for granting an annulment is "incapacity to assume the obligations" of marriage. The majority of these cases consist of people with personality characteristics directly opposed to those of marriage. For example, a person with a narcissistic personality is deemed incapable of entering into the marriage relationship, which is directed toward the good of another. The Catholic church's pronouncement is in unequivocal agreement with Scripture: pride makes love impossible.

According to Scripture, one's love for God cannot exceed one's love for human beings who were created in his image (1 John 4:20). The same test applies to humility. The true measure of humility is not what is shown to God in prayer but what is demonstrated to others on

---

29. James F. Collins, "TF Translates DNA into Music Sequence," *The Harvard Crimson*, April 26, 2007, accessed April 7, 2015, http://www.thecrimson.com/article/2007/4/26/tf-translates-dna-into-music-sequence/.

a daily basis. This is the measuring rod used to separate the sheep from the goats.

> "When the Son of Man comes in his glory, and all the angels with him, he will sit on his glorious throne. All the nations will be gathered before him, and he will separate the people one from another as a shepherd separates the sheep from the goats. He will put the sheep on his right and the goats on his left. Then the King will say to those on his right, 'Come, you who are blessed by my Father; take your inheritance, the kingdom prepared for you since the creation of the world. For I was hungry and you gave me something to eat, I was thirsty and you gave me something to drink, I was a stranger and you invited me in, I needed clothes and you clothed me, I was sick and you looked after me, I was in prison and you came to visit me.' Then the righteous will answer him, 'Lord, when did we see you hungry and feed you, or thirsty and give you something to drink? When did we see you a stranger and invite you in, or needing clothes and clothe you? When did we see you sick or in prison and go to visit you?' The King will reply, 'Truly I tell you, whatever you did for one of the least of these brothers and sisters of mine, you did for me.' (Matthew 25:31-40)

It takes great humility to love the lowliest, the outcast, the shunned, and the sinner. This is the very humility of Christ. It is the litmus test that weeds out the true from the false, the righteous from the wicked, the counterfeit from the real. The root of the Tree of the Knowledge of Good and Evil is pride. It is pride which reveals itself as the desire for independence and the desire to receive human accolades.

The true and the false, the counterfeit and the real, are differentiated based on the kingdom of origin, the root, or the spiritual source of the power. Unfortunately, the source is a spiritual one—it cannot be visually seen. True faith can be heard. It has a sound that emanates from the

Father's heart and is in harmony with heaven. Jesus taught his disciples about the "fruit" which would differentiate the good trees from the bad. That fruit, according to Jesus, consisted of words, which were reflective of the heart.

> No good tree bears bad fruit, nor does a bad tree bear good fruit. Each tree is recognized by its own fruit. People do not pick figs from thorn bushes, or grapes from briers. A good man brings good things out of the good stored up in his heart, and an evil man brings evil things out of the evil stored up in his heart. For the mouth speaks what the heart is full of. (Luke 6:43-45)

The lack of humility precludes love, the only attribute by which Christ declared his disciples would be known (John 13:35). Everything we say about ourselves or about each other must flow out of humility. In other words, heaven has a sound. That sound is the sound of humility. The sound of heaven is the testimony of Jesus. The role of every disciple of Christ, every child of God, is not only to hold to the testimony of Jesus but also to release it here on earth. That testimony is the sound of genuine love that comes from humility. Devoid of love, one is devoid of God's sound, devoid of God's identity, and, ultimately, devoid of good fruit. Without love, it is impossible to release the sound of heaven. Without love, there is no song, only noise.

> If I speak in the tongues of men or of angels, but do not have love, I am only a resounding gong or a clanging cymbal. If I have the gift of prophecy and can fathom all mysteries and all knowledge, and if I have a faith that can move mountains, but do not have love, I am nothing. If I give all I possess to the poor and give over my body to hardship that I may boast, but do not have love, I gain nothing. (1 Corinthians 13:1-3)

The Giving Tree

Humility is the process by which one decreases so the Holy Spirit can increase. By the Holy Spirit, a child of God can speak the words of heaven and thereby release the glory of heaven in signs, wonders, and miracles. However, humility cannot be gained by accumulating information, nor can it be channeled through religious activity. The only source of humility is an encounter with the glory of God. Humility comes only through relationship and experience. To know God in the biblical understanding is to experience him. That experience, in turn, results in humility.

John Wimber, a man through whom God did great healing miracles, learned firsthand the value God places on humility. For ten months, Wimber remained obedient to the Lord's instructions to pray for healing while nothing happened. Wimber writes, "I was purged of my pride and self-sufficiency. I was humiliated, and I was humbled. God had to cleanse a vessel before it was fit to fill with his precious oil of healing. I believe God began healing the sick through me only after I came to a place of total dependence on his grace and mercy."[30]

The Hallelujah Chorus

George Frideric Handel, with tears streaming down his face, cried out, "I did think I did see all heaven before me, and the great God Himself." He had just completed writing what would be known throughout history as the "Hallelujah Chorus." Handel had struggled financially all of his life. His experience was one failure after another.

On April 8, 1741—with failing health and on the verge of complete financial ruin—Handel gave what he considered to be his farewell concert. A few months later, a friend gave him a libretto based on the life of Christ. Handel set to composing on August 22, and in the short span of twenty-four days, Handel filled 260 pages of manuscript. One of Handel's biographers stated, "Considering the immensity of the work, and the short time involved, it will remain, perhaps forever, the greatest feat in the whole history of music composition."

---

30. John Wimber and Kevin Springer, *Power Healing* (New York, NY: HarperCollins, 1987), 54.

Grace Notes from Heaven

In composing what he would later call the "Messiah," Handel stayed housebound for three weeks, quoting the words of Paul, "Whether I was in the body or out of my body when I wrote it, I know not." Not long after this, Handel's fortunes increased greatly and remained constant until his death. Handel once said about his audiences, "My Lord, I should be sorry if I only entertain them. I wish to make them better."

Jesus said, "Very truly I tell you, whoever believes in me will do the works I have been doing, and they will do even greater things than these, because I am going to the Father" (John 14:12). Over the two and a half centuries since its composition, Handel's Messiah's performances have fed the hungry, clothed the naked, fostered the orphan, and done more to relieve human suffering than any other musical production in history.

Created to be Sounded

The new covenant ushered in a new relationship with God in which the Holy Spirit would reside in every believer. This is the "Christ in you, the hope of glory" (Colossians 1:27). The word *glory* is closely related to light. Since light and sound consist of the same elements, *glory* is related to both light and sound. Christ in you, the hope of *glory*, is not only the hope of being "lighted," but also "sounded." In his theological discourse with the Samaritan woman at the well, Jesus explained that the Father was seeking those who would worship him in Spirit and truth. Jesus was describing the heart of the new covenant relationship with God. Thus, the new covenant relationship opened the way for all of the children of God to "be sounded" or released as the sound of heaven on earth. The disciples gathered together in one accord and waited for the promised Holy Spirit. As the Holy Spirit came upon them, they were *sounded*:

> When the Day of Pentecost had fully come, they were all with one accord in one place. And suddenly there came a sound from heaven, as of a rushing mighty wind, and it filled the whole house where they were sitting. Then there appeared to them divided tongues, as of fire, and

The Giving Tree

one sat upon each of them. And they were all filled with the Holy Spirit and began to speak with other tongues, as the Spirit gave them utterance. (Acts 2:1-4 NKJV)

The empowerment by the Holy Spirit at Pentecost was, according to Scripture, the fulfillment of God's promise in Joel: "I will pour out my Spirit on all people. Your sons and daughters will prophesy...and everyone who calls on the name of the Lord will be saved" (Acts 2:17, 21). To prophesy means to speak the very words of God. To say what God is saying is to release the sound of heaven on earth. This can only be done by the power of the Holy Spirit. The book of Acts is full of references to the Holy Spirit witnessing through obedient believers. Jesus commissioned his disciples to preach the kingdom, heal the sick, drive out demons, and raise the dead—all primarily with words. To do this is to hold to the testimony of Jesus. Every believer in Christ is called to live as a son or daughter of the living God, to be a disciple of Christ, and to release heaven wherever they go.

The children of God depend on him for everything because they know and trust in his faithfulness. Jesus did nothing apart from the will of God. The same is true of all of God's children. They choose not to "live on bread alone but on every word that comes from the mouth of God." Intimate knowledge of who God is and who they are in Christ enables them to cease striving and rest in his goodness. They know what it means to be a friend of God, and they can serve others as Christ served—even when it is done to the least of these. A submitted will declares, *"Father...not my will but yours be done,"* even when God's will implies hardship and pain. The hallmarks of a submitted will are love and humility. These are the marks of a true disciple of Christ.

The word of God is always fresh. There is always fresh bread from heaven, a fresh word, fresh revelation of who Jesus was, is, and will always be. This is the destiny of the children of God and the disciples of Christ—to reveal God's glory throughout the earth, and the primary means of this revelation is through sound. The leaves of the tree of life are always green regardless of season, for the presence of God does not depend on season but on a heart ready to do his will. The testimonies of God are ours to keep, but to keep God's testimonies does not mean to own. To keep the testimonies of God means to steward them, which means to share them widely, keep them constantly on our lips as teaching for the next generation, and release faith in those who hear. The mouth of a child of God is made to be filled with God's glory and then to release it in words. These words consist of God's promises in Scripture, prophetic words, and the testimonies of what God is doing.

These testimonies are not for the glory of the people through whom or to whom the mighty acts were done, but are exclusively for the revelation of his unchanging nature. The testimonies of God keep the nature of God at the forefront of thought, the focus of attention, and dispel error. They declare his goodness, love, and his continuing presence against the voices that claim otherwise.

> When people hear about what God used to do, some of the things they say is: "Oh, that was a very long time ago....I thought it was God that did it. Has God changed? Is he not an immutable God, the same yesterday, today, and forever? Does not that furnish an argument to prove that what God has done at one time he can do at another?" Nay, I think I may push it a little further, and say what he has done once is a prophecy of what he intends to do again…Whatever God has done…is to be looked upon as a precedent….[Let us] with earnestness see that God would restore to us the faith of the men of old, that we may richly enjoy his grace as in the days of old.[31]

A child of God is called to release a sound, and that sound is the sound of faith. Faith is hearing the word of God and responding appropriately. To do this requires an inclined ear, ever hearing, ever listening to what the Holy Spirit is saying, and ready to respond. That response is in both word and deed, which work in tandem. Jesus exercised his

---

31. Charles Spurgeon, accessed April 7, 2015, http://www.spurgeon.org/sermons/0263.htm.

authority through words. The same is true of his disciples. Signs, wonders, and miracles done in the name of Jesus Christ are all evidence of the truth of who Jesus is. These signs are the witness of the Holy Spirit which follow his disciples wherever they go.

Jesus gave them not only the power of the Holy Spirit to be his witnesses, but he also entrusted them with his authority. The disciples of Jesus Christ operate under the delegated authority of Jesus, who is Lord over all. Authority is the right to use power. The point of delegated authority is critical, as with great authority comes great responsibility. Jesus did not give the disciples carte blanche to do whatever they wished with his authority and power. They were called to hold to his testimony, remain rooted in love, and maintain a close relationship with him, just as Jesus maintained intimacy with the Father while on earth. As is demonstrated in the story of Jesus' encounter with the Centurion, authority is exercised through words.

> He was not far from the house when the centurion sent friends to say to him: "Lord, don't trouble yourself, for I do not deserve to have you come under my roof. That is why I did not even consider myself worthy to come to you. But say the word, and my servant will be healed. For I myself am a man under authority, with soldiers under me. I tell this one, 'Go,' and he goes; and that one, 'Come,' and he comes. I say to my servant, 'Do this,' and he does it." When Jesus heard this, he was amazed at him, and turning to the crowd following him, he said, "I tell you, I have not found such great faith even in Israel." Then the men who had been sent returned to the house and found the servant well. (Luke 7:6-10)

True Authority Originates in Humility

The key to walking in the legitimate authority of Jesus Christ is humility. Humility, in turn, only comes from intimacy with Christ. True authority is never used to manipulate or control. True authority can never be based on a formula but flows out of relationship because it reflects the Father's heart. It listens to what the Holy Spirit is saying, sees what he sees, and then says what he says. Because true authority is exercised from the place of humility, it will never seek its own gain, but will only seek to bring glory and honor to Jesus. In the same way, Jesus did not seek his own glory, but gave all glory to the Father.

Over and over through the book of Acts we hear the same basic message: "The word of the Lord grew and multiplied." The disciples were called to proclaim the kingdom of God and to demonstrate it by healing the sick, raising the dead, and driving out demons. In other words, Jesus sent them out with his authority as King over all to take dominion over every place they set their feet. They were sent out to reclaim for God both the land and the people. With a word and in the name of Jesus, demons were driven out, blind eyes were opened, and the lame walked. The disciples walked in the authority of Jesus Christ. The testimonies of the miracles done through the risen Christ went out, and people believed and were saved. The word of God bears fruit in all seasons. A word from a child of God bears fruit because it carries the sound of God and his intent. Furthermore, it is empowered by the Holy Spirit and given under the authority of Jesus Christ.

A disciple of Christ needs to be ever listening so he or she can hear what God is saying, see what God sees, and then say what he says. While he was being stoned to death, Stephen saw Jesus at the right hand of God. He then uttered the very words of forgiveness which Jesus said from the cross. Stephen saw heaven and released what he saw as a sound on earth. The power of redemption was released into the life of Saul, who watched over Stephen's death. Stephen's words were seeds of power, setting the persecutor Saul on the beginning of the journey into his destiny as the apostle Paul.

> But Stephen, full of the Holy Spirit, looked up to heaven
> and saw the glory of God, and Jesus standing at the right

The Giving Tree

hand of God. "Look," he said, "I see heaven open and the Son of Man standing at the right hand of God."

At this they covered their ears and, yelling at the top of their voices, they all rushed at him, dragged him out of the city and began to stone him. Meanwhile, the witnesses laid their coats at the feet of a young man named Saul. While they were stoning him, Stephen prayed, "Lord Jesus, receive my spirit." Then he fell on his knees and cried out, "Lord, do not hold this sin against them." When he had said this, he fell asleep. (Acts 7:55-60)

The sound of heaven is the sound of unity. Heaven is filled with the sound of a "great multitude" (Revelation 19:1, 6). When the sound of the Father's heart is the sound released by God's people, then heaven will be released on earth. The greatest evangelistic force on the earth is a unified church, a church that is not silent but declares God's wonders in every language (Acts 2:11). When the throne of God—not the pulpit—is the center of the church, and the desire for God's manifest presence replaces the desire for the anointing, then true unity will take place in the body of Christ.

Each believer in Christ was created to "be sounded," to sing a song in harmony with the heart of God, a love song as it were. The sound of heaven is a song of love; the song of the Bridegroom to his bride; the song of the Lamb slain before the foundation of the world. It is a blood song; the song of the shed blood of Jesus Christ on the cross. This is the common unifying thread through the entire body of Christ—the Father's love song in the shed blood of Jesus. Paul knew that song and pledged to know nothing but "Jesus Christ and him crucified" (1 Corinthians 2:2). As the bride of Christ, our song must be in harmony with heaven. The church must stay unified in song so that our effectiveness isn't compromised. Paul accentuates this in 1 Corinthians 14:8 when he says, "If the trumpet does not sound a clear call, who will get ready for battle?"

During his earthly ministry, Jesus didn't leave the atmosphere as he found it. The spirit of prophecy, which is the testimony of Jesus, is to release the sound of hope in place of despair, the sound of life in place of death, the sound of healing in place of brokenness, and the sound of freedom in place of bondage. When the people of God are in tune with the heart of God, they have the potential to release the sound of God into lives and circumstances. They have the power to bring heaven to earth. The sound of heaven on earth is the sound of a unified bride.

Handel was viciously attacked by England's church for most of his life, mainly because he wrote biblical dramas to be performed in secular theaters. When the Messiah premiered on April 13, 1742, the King of England attended, in spite of the controversy. As the first notes of the "Hallelujah Chorus" rang out, the king rose to his feet, prompting the entire audience to stand also due to royal protocol. This tradition to stand for the "Hallelujah Chorus" has been practiced over two hundred years.

Every son and daughter of God is called to release the sound of heaven. That sound is the sound of the Father's heart, the love song of heaven. This sound is the sound of faith, the sound of the Christian witness. This sound causes situations to change, healing to come, and miracles to happen. This sound releases the glory of God, the power of God, the goodness of God, and the fruit of God. It reverberates throughout the earth, harmonizes those within its reach, causes walls to fall, and earthly kings to stand.

> Then I heard what sounded like a great multitude, like the roar of rushing waters and like loud peals of thunder, shouting: "Hallelujah! For our Lord God Almighty reigns." (Revelation 19:6)

8

A New Song for the Bride

The Gospel According to a Modern Ruth

Discipleship is not a program and it is not a formula. It is not linear and predictable. It is dynamic, multidimensional, organic, and alive. Discipleship is a lifestyle. It cannot be sectioned off, contained, or put in a box, just as God himself cannot be put into a box. Discipleship is a picture, a parable, a story, a gospel. God's sound can be examined only in the context of discipleship where people become living examples of God's "sound-makers" as they go about the Lord's business on a daily basis. Therefore, the study of God's sound breaks all the rules, and it colors outside all the lines.

The following are excerpts from in-depth interviews, testimonies recorded in personal journals, and eyewitness accounts of miracles and personal transformations. Together they comprise a summary report of thirteen years of action research. The evidence presented here consists of stories of an extraordinary God working miracles both in and through the lives of ordinary people.

The story of what God has done through our ministry Giving Tree—also known as Bread of Life through our feeding programs—is distinctly not about numbers. It has not been about achieving a critical mass of disciples or people to achieve a well-thought-out and predetermined goal.

The Giving Tree

Quite the opposite has been the case. The journey has been a difficult one, and the attrition rate has been quite large due to both financial and family hardships and the challenge of being still and waiting on God.

What has astonished many is the fact that so much has been done through so few. The core group from the outset has consisted of four committed disciples through whom God touches thousands of people weekly. This is not without biblical precedent. Jesus had twelve disciples whose legacy impacted the world. David had three mighty men, each of whom could overcome hundreds. Gideon was specifically instructed to reduce his army's size so that victory would be attributable to God alone and not to human effort. Giving Tree is a story of faith and commitment. The four of us have, from the beginning, focused on our relationship with Jesus and steadfastly relied on the Holy Spirit rather than on our own strength. With all of its component branches, Giving Tree has been built "not by might, nor by power, but by the Holy Spirit" (Zechariah 4:6).

Giving Tree has not possessed many of the material resources which most churches would consider obligatory. We have not had access to a traditional church building where large groups of Christians could gather and house many programs and activities. Instead, we have been grateful for our "child's lunch," maximizing the use of our home and dedicating it to the Lord for his purposes. The lack of a building has exposed us to ridicule over the years and caused many to label us a "Bible study" rather than a church. The absence of a traditional pulpit has also given some people reason to believe they had a license to dishonor the church and me personally. While not having access to a building or vast amounts of resources has been very difficult and painful at times, it has, in retrospect, been the source of tremendous blessing.

Of necessity, we have learned that the essence of being a disciple of Christ is to have an encounter with the risen Christ; that worship is not about a place—not Mount Gerizim, Jerusalem, or any church building—but about worshiping the Father in Spirit and in truth. The "lack" of a building has facilitated our understanding of the divine mandate

A New Song for the Bride

to take dominion over the land and the territory we live in. In the marketplace, we proclaim the message of the kingdom daily and demonstrate it in grocery stores, clothing stores, on the streets, in shelters, and everywhere imaginable. We have become witnesses for Christ in our hometown, reclaiming it for his glory, multiplying, and leaving a lasting legacy in our wake.

We have been obligated to cooperate with others, learn firsthand the value of stewardship, generosity, and the widow's mite. As a result, we have close relationships with the public schools, law enforcement, local business organizations, the media, and local and state government agencies. Instead of focusing on the maintenance of a building and the garnering of both people and finances to that end, we have put our efforts toward deepening our relationship with the Lord and being obedient to his voice. Our mission's success has been undeterred by our "lack" of a building but has, instead, been ensured by the presence of the Lord with us.

In the American church, the standards of measurement and the values by which professing Christians guide their lives are borrowed from the world and culture in which they are immersed. In other words, the world is in the church. Unfortunately, our standards are not God's standards. This is the modern analogue to the expectations of the Jews of Jesus' time that the Messiah would usher in an earthly kingdom. These expectations blinded the Jews to the miracles of Jesus and deafened them to the message of a Messiah whose kingdom was distinctly not of this world. A kingdom "not of this world," therefore, demands an otherworldly paradigm of measurement. According to Jesus, heaven declares the least the greatest and the last to be the first.

At present, Jesus is betrothed to a bride who does not share his value system. This means she does not esteem what he esteems, she does not disdain what he disdains, and her heart does not break for the things that break his heart. Such a marriage cannot and will not stand. Yet there is hope for this bride, for God himself has declared that she will, in fact, learn to love what he loves, adore what he adores, and do only what she sees him doing (see Ephesians 5:27).

The Giving Tree

The conclusion drawn from our team's accumulated years of experience gained on the American mission field is that a biblical paradigm for discipleship requires a shift to align with the value system of heaven. God's kingdom is ushered in, in its entirety, and that includes a value system. As opposed to a program or curriculum, a value system transcends time, generation, culture, race, and gender. While a program is bound by all of these restrictions and is prone to obsolescence, a value system is boundless, cross-cultural, cross-generational, cross-racial, and timeless.

Value Number One: Human Value Is Inherent

God greatly enjoys pouring his power and favor on the unlikely; the people deemed worthless and unusable. Human value in the kingdom of God is inherent. It is not earned, not relative, and does not involve either position or status. Instead, it is absolute, finding its derivation in the recognition that each human being, regardless of race, gender, economic status, and worldly significance, has inherent value as a divine image-bearer. Kingdom value collides with earthly value on every level. The sound of God declares that God is love, I am loved, and others are equally loved by God. It facilitates a shift in perspective and a change in sight to reveal value in people and places the world deems both worthless and useless. In God's kingdom, the offer to be a child of God, to have a voice, and to "be sounded" for his glory, the offer of the new covenant relationship excludes no one.

The concept of inherent value is applicable both inside the church and out in the marketplace. Giving Tree is the story of the church's functioning as a living, breathing organism—a building constructed from living stones. We had to be amenable to be taught and guided by the Holy Spirit, available and open to his leading, and ones who allow Jesus and Jesus alone to be the cornerstone. Our church without walls demanded that we relinquish our desires, our opinions, and our preconceived ideas of "church" and let Jesus build his church according to the principles of his kingdom. The biblical view of the church as comprised of living stones has contributed to forming covenant relationships. Our commitment to each other through both valley and mountaintop

A New Song for the Bride

experiences has stood firm. We carry one another's burdens and rejoice when one is blessed. We have learned to treasure the gift of the body of Christ, to understand that the whole is greater than the sum of its parts, and that relationships are neither optional nor disposable.

> But Ruth replied, "Don't urge me to leave you or to turn back from you. Where you go I will go, and where you stay I will stay. Your people will be my people and your God my God. Where you die I will die, and there I will be buried. May the Lord deal with me, be it ever so severely, if even death separates you and me." When Naomi realized that Ruth was determined to go with her, she stopped urging her. (Ruth 1:16-18)

Ruth clung to Naomi and chose to see value where the world declared there was none. Ruth's commitment was risky and costly, involving an uncertain future in a foreign land ruled by an unfamiliar God and inhabited by unfamiliar people. More than a thousand years before Christ, Ruth proved herself a friend of God, fulfilling the command of Jesus to his disciples, "Love each other as I have loved you. Greater love has no one than this: to lay down one's life for one's friends" (John 15:12-13). Love demonstrated through covenant relationships is the hallmark of the disciple and friend of Jesus, who is then privy to the Father's business.

Outside of the church, the Holy Spirit's repeated message has been that "one is enough"—one person is enough, and one square mile is enough. Jesus "had" to go through Samaria to save one Samaritan woman. The Lord has expected us to do likewise. We have focused on "the one" rather than on the numbers. Our congregants now number in the thousands, the majority of whom are located outside the church walls. This requires a willingness to be inconvenienced and venture out of our way to modern-day Samaria—New York City, the Bronx, Vermont, etc.—to seek out and save the one lost sheep.

***

The Giving Tree

Jacob

During one of our many ministry trips, I became aware of a young boy who had been born without eyes and ears and with only a partial nose. I had seen countless healing miracles by this time and was confident that God could and would do another. I asked the local people who knew the family to convey my desire to pray for Jacob and, within a very brief period, the appointment was set at a local church.

As I was praying before the prayer ministry with Jacob and inquired for the guidance of the Holy Spirit, I heard the Lord clearly say to me, "You are not to break any curses off this child." I found that a bit strange but agreed, and I received no other instructions on how or what to pray for Jacob at that time. Although I had Jacob's condition described to me by many people, I was unprepared for the boy who sat before me in his stroller. As I looked at him, my heart broke. Truly he had been born with no eyes nor ears, and had only one nostril. How would I let him know how much God loves him? I always speak to the people to whom I minister, quote Scripture, and tell them of God's love. Here, however, was a seemingly impossible wall of silence between Jacob and me.

Then I felt the Holy Spirit tell me to pick him up and hold him. "Of course, I thought, in agreement. There is still touch." I picked him up and began to pray, to sing, and simply to love him. I held him, rocked him, and prayed for God to give him beautiful big blue eyes and to free him from the prison of his own body. Jacob was making some grunting sounds during this.

His mother said, "He likes that. He likes what you are doing."

I was pleased that Jacob and I had connected by the power of the Holy Spirit. I put him down, though, disappointed. There was no miracle. No ears appeared, no nose, nothing at all that I could detect. This was not at all what I expected. Then I kept hearing the Holy Spirit say, "I am going to use Jacob as a vessel for my healing."

"I am not going to tell his mother that," I retorted. "That is absurd when this boy needs so much healing himself." The problem was that I kept hearing those words repeated over and over, so finally, I relented.

I reluctantly turned to the mother and said, "I know this is going to sound a bit bizarre, but I believe the Lord is saying he is going to use Jacob to heal others."

Thankfully, instead of being insulted, she simply replied, "That makes sense. The last time a pastor prayed for him, nothing happened to Jacob, but the pastor was healed of his illness. By the way, thank you for not breaking any curses off him. When prayer ministers see Jacob, that is the first thing they do. I told myself, if you started doing that too, I would take Jacob and leave."

I was shocked and had no answers for anything that was happening. I was on my way out when the mother said, "Jacob wants to pray for you."

"All right," I acquiesced, all the while wondering exactly how that was going to work. I returned from the ladies' room, and the mother was smiling broadly. "Jacob's prayer for you is that your hair would shine with the glory of the Lord," she proudly announced.

"What?" I exclaimed, stunned. "How could he possibly know that?"

"Know what?" inquired the mother.

"My hair is very curly and very hard to manage. I have never been very happy with it, so I pray a prayer I have never shared with anyone. I told the Lord I am not so happy with his choice of curly hair for me, but if I have to keep it, then could he please make it shine with his glory?

I left the church that day, having seen no great miracles of physical healing. Nothing had happened as I had expected. More than that, I was left wondering who had ministered to whom.

***

Sarah

Sarah has been one of the pillars of Giving Tree since its inception. She has persevered in the face of many who have told her that she has no place in the ministry and no place serving God. She has gone from a stranger to a relationship with Jesus to the Father's princess who spends countless hours in prayer, selflessly interceding for others and helping to carry their burdens. She is kind and gentle in spirit, and I could not have made this journey without her prayers and support. This is the beginning of Sarah's story. Sarah is, most definitely, "Daddy's little girl."

The Giving Tree

For as long as I can remember, I struggled with a desire to be loved, affirmed, and to know that I was good enough.

I felt this longing in my heart for more. God knew the answer to my heart's cry and sent me to Sherri's house one cold January morning in 2007 for a cup of coffee. I grew up in a home with religion but not relationship. I didn't even know that regular people like me could have a relationship with Jesus. I thought that was reserved for the priests and pastors, important people that God had chosen.

While there, she prayed for me. It was not like any of the specific prayers I prayed in church my whole life. It was intimate and personal. She asked Jesus to come and be with us, and he did. Sherri explained to me that Jesus speaks to us in many different ways, and one of those ways can be a picture. The Lord gave her a few pictures for me that day. The first picture was of a scene that was going on in my family. It was actually something that had just happened the week before with my husband and son and me. There was no way she could have known that. Next, the Lord showed her a picture of the five people in my family, each standing in separate silos, and he showed her that I was dressed as a shepherd. Now she had my attention. I kept my secret pain and longing of my heart to myself. How could she have known this? I was sobbing at this point.

The final picture was a picture of Jesus standing at the door of my heart and knocking. The Lord says, "Here I am, I stand at the door and knock, if you hear my voice and open the door, I will come in." At that moment, I knew it was Jesus. That he was really there and wanted me to know him. I knew that the longing in my heart was for him. So I asked him into my heart with tears rolling down my cheeks, and my life has not been the same since!

***

Minhee

I thought it was a typical Saturday evening as I arranged the notes on the podium, preparing for my class in divine healing. I glanced up for a moment and squinted in the faint light to focus on a new student in the class who had quietly slipped in without a word and taken a seat in

A New Song for the Bride

the back. I could barely discern the features belonging to a petite Asian woman hunched down in her chair as if in an attempt to be invisible.

At this, the Holy Spirit spoke into my spirit, "Do not look at what you see. She is a butterfly."

This was the beginning of my friendship with Minhee, who is one of the founding members of Giving Tree, and whose Korean name means "lady in the sky." Such a name rings of nobility, hope, joy, and blessing. A graduate of both Cornell and Harvard, few would guess her incredible battle with depression. As I would later learn, Minhee struggled with low self-esteem for most of her life. When she walked into my class that evening, she was at a particularly low point as her mother had recently passed away, a mother who wanted a noble lady as a daughter and had named her accordingly. This is her story.

> My poor mom was so baffled by her tomboy, no-makeup-wearing daughter who dressed poorly, regarded herself as ugly and deserving of nothing, and treated herself as such. All of my life, she begged me to treat myself well so others would treat me well too. I just didn't seem to care much about myself. Depression plagued me from childhood. I always told her that I didn't care about myself and my life, and I know this brought her much pain.
>
> As a little girl, I wondered why we were on this earth. I didn't understand the point of life, and I started to get very depressed. I got so depressed my mom took me to a psychiatrist, and my grades dropped to Ds and an F my junior year of high school.
>
> With those grades, my dream of going to Cornell seemed impossible, and I became even more depressed. But God was not done with this story. He brought me a wonderful mentor who helped me win a Westinghouse Science Competition award. Shortly after notifying Cornell of this award, I received an acceptance letter, a couple of months before the official letters were sent out. With 1180 (out of 1600) SAT score, and Ds and a F on my junior year transcript, I was admitted to Cornell by the grace of God.
>
> At Cornell, I could barely handle the workload. Depression hit again so hard that I took my second semester freshman year off. But this time

was different because of a friend who shared Jesus with me, and I came to believe in his love. The Lord gave me a strategy for studying: to stop doing my homework and instead use my energy to concentrate on the professor's lectures. My grades began to improve.

After Cornell, I wanted to study at Harvard Graduate School of Education, but I was hesitant to apply. Although my later semesters showed great improvements, my beginning grades at Cornell were dismal, and my practice GRE scores were not good. At that time, GREs consisted of filling in bubbles with a pencil. Questions left blank were marked as wrong answers, so it was to my advantage to put something down. A few minutes before time was up, I had about a third of the test remaining, so I began filling in all the bubbles with "D, D, D, D, etc.," until the end. Then for some reason, a minute before time was up, I changed my mind and erased all those D's and instead marked them all with "B." Once again, by God's grace, I got a miraculously good GRE score and, with that, applied to Harvard.

I was not a strong writer, so my application essay to Harvard had three glued-in photographs of me doing volunteer work in France, Haiti, and Korea. I got an acceptance letter to Harvard several months before official acceptance letters went out. Again, with a mediocre college transcript (including some C's and D's), a God-given GRE score, and a few pictures, God made it happen. His destiny and direction for a person's life cannot be stopped no matter the grades or SAT scores.

I also had high levels of the Hepatitis B virus antigens and high levels of the antibodies that combat the antigens. I was told this was medically impossible, and my doctor was aware of only two other cases in the world involving this condition. My doctor said I do not have to write on any medical forms that I had a preexisting condition of Hepatitis B because they might not understand the lab result.

I was physically and emotionally very ill when I was diagnosed with chronic Hepatitis B, which is medically incurable. My mother decided that I should forgo the weekly shots and wait to see how the disease developed. Shortly after that, I began to juice and care about myself, my health, and my nutrition. The Lord healed me at the same time I started to care about myself. This was a process of changing my diet over the years and of caring for myself. My blood work eventually showed my Hepatitis B to be cured. "You are what doctors call a medical miracle.

A New Song for the Bride

You were a Hepatitis B carrier, but now it's as if you had the vaccination. Your body developed the immunity," my doctor informed me.

In August 2012, I had to leave my job abruptly. I was terrified about my finances and about health insurance, but I felt God strongly telling me not to get another job. I didn't tell anyone because it was crazy. How would I pay my bills? I felt him saying instead of a normal job that I was to start some sort of business. Also, I kept telling God that I just wanted to build something with him. For several months I just kept repeatedly hearing, "Don't get a job, and start a business." But I still did not tell anyone.

On January 27, 2013, Sherri called to tell me that she felt God was saying that 1) He did not want me to get a conventional job; 2) That I was to start something entrepreneurial; 3) That I would help build something with him. I was so utterly amazed I almost dropped the phone. This is how I became a part of Giving Tree.

A couple of years ago, Minhee had a dream about starting an organizing business called Clutter Free-dom. Some questioned her pricing, some the ill-placed hyphen in the business name, others thought the entire idea was ludicrous. Nevertheless, she forged ahead in the face of opposition, believing it was an idea given by the Lord. Once shy and reticent to speak, she now goes into some of the wealthiest parts of Manhattan to help people organize their apartments, pray for their healing, and share the good news of the kingdom of God with strangers. The demand for her services outstrips capacity, and clients often offer to pay more than the requested fee. The opposition has been silenced and astonished by what the Lord has done. Truly, Minhee is a butterfly. Gone is the tomboy who cared little about herself. Minhee is now a courageous woman of God who cares about both herself and others. She has become worthy of her name: Lady in the Sky.

***

The Giving Tree

Barth

It was Christmastime, and, as usual, I was a little late sending our Christmas cards. I was waiting in line at the post office to buy stamps, when I caught a glimpse of a boy standing with his mother at the front of the line. The boy's head was somewhat misshapen, and his clothes were rumpled. As I watched him standing there quietly next to his mother, I heard the Holy Spirit tell me to pray for him.

Now the line was very long, and I had already waited quite a while to get toward the front where I now stood, so I was very reluctant to get out of line. "Lord," I objected, "I need to get my stamps first. Then I will pray." I stubbornly stood my ground against the leading of the Holy Spirit. When I had finally made my purchase, I turned to find that the boy and his mother had disappeared. Instantly, conviction seized my heart. "Lord, I am sorry. I just wanted to get my stamps. If you still want me to pray for him, please provide another opportunity."

As I left the post office, the boy and his mother were standing next to the post office boxes. I approached the mother, introduced myself, and asked permission to pray for her son. She didn't seem to have great confidence that anything good would come out of it but agreed nonetheless. After asking his name, I turned to the boy and asked, "Hello, Barth, my name is Sherri, and I am a Christian minister, and I am going to pray for you. Would that be okay?" Barth nodded. "Barth, do you know Jesus?"

At that point, everything changed. Barth answered with the utmost confidence of one who truly knows Jesus, "Yes, I do. Jesus is Lord!" His face broke out in a big smile, and it lit up with the glory of the Lord. To this day, I have never heard anyone answer the question about knowing Jesus with such confidence. While I prayed for Barth's physical healing, the sense that this was backward never left me. I turned to the mother and said, "I believe that your son has much to share and to give other people. He knows—really knows—Jesus." I do not think she believed me as she just shook her head in a manner that said, "What a nut." Then she took her precious son and walked away. As for me, I walked away changed.

***

A New Song for the Bride

Banquet on the Beach

In the spring of 2015, three of us independently heard the Lord tell us that he wanted us to serve a banquet for the poor on the beach in Rye. Rye is an affluent community located in Westchester County, New York, one of the wealthiest and most expensive places to live in the United States. The Lord told us that this banquet was about releasing the sound of praise and worship. We all struggled with what we heard for several reasons. The first was expense. We believed that the Lord wanted us to rent the pavilion on the beach, the cost of which was approximately $500 for half a day. Further complicating matters were the logistics of getting the poor to the beach and the eventual reception they would face from others when they arrived.

However, as we stepped out in obedience, it was clear that the Lord's favor was on the event. The town of Rye was more supportive than we could have ever imagined. When they questioned why we wanted to host the dinner on the beach, we simply explained that the poor deserve to be treated with dignity and need to know they have value as human beings. The price was cut in half. Tables, chairs, and a grill were provided. Restaurants donated food. Families and individuals cooked and provided all that we needed. The only mistake in the whole process was my own.

When the Lord said that the banquet was about the sound of praise going forth, I immediately assumed we needed a worship band. We have a very simple church and do not have a worship team. Therefore, I began to contact all of my pastor friends and everyone I knew to see if we could get a worship team to play. It was very odd. Several people agreed and then backed out. Even the day of the event, someone had agreed to come and then texted in the middle of the banquet to say he would not be coming. The problem was that I had heard something but misunderstood its meaning.

A bit disheartened and wondering whether I had heard the Lord correctly, I stood watching the people enjoy their dinner. We decided to play "canned music" as we had nothing else. Suddenly, a woman stood up and began to sing with the music, then a second, a third, and a high school boy began asking for the name of the song that was playing. All at once, I understood that I had been wrong. God had not wanted a professional worship team. He did not want entertainment. He wanted worship—simple worship from the heart, and he wanted everyone involved. This was a banquet to demonstrate that everyone has value in God's eyes and that all are invited to the King's banquet. It was also to show that everyone is created to release a sound—God's sound—which both brings him glory and releases glory.

***

Christopher

The college entrance process is difficult for any parent, but for our family, it was more so as it has reopened old wounds and moved to the forefront of our minds the role of God as Father. When my ex-husband disappeared from our family into Russia five years previously, he took all of our finances with him, including our children's college fund. In our affluent community, parents saved for years to ensure their children would be able to attend the best colleges. How does one enter into the college process without constant consideration that there is no money to pay? The application process is intense, filled with seemingly endless standardized testing, fees, resume crafting, and the chance of eventual admittance into a "top" college in the single digits. Secretly hidden in the deep recesses of my heart was the unrelenting pressure due to unanswered financial questions related to my son's college education. This burden was not my son's to bear. It was mine; at least it should have been.

My son, Christopher, struggled with self-confidence throughout the application process. He would sit for hours in front of the computer with only the blinking cursor disrupting the screen's empty space. In regular two-hour intervals, I would walk by to see the progress of one single line gracing the otherwise blank page that would need to be filled not once but many times over for the next ten college applications. How does one trust God in a process that runs so counter to everything in the kingdom and which has the potential to devastate or affirm a child's personal worth? Even when the pages were eventually filled with the intellect and soul of this precious seventeen-year-old, what is the guarantee that anyone on the receiving end will really see beyond the statistics to the person he is?

A New Song for the Bride

The exploration of the role of God's sound reinforced for me the power inherent in testimony. On Friday, September 25, 2015, I requested that Minhee share her college testimony with Christopher. Both of my sons were perplexed at the knowledge that Minhee, someone so supremely "unqualified" to gain entrance to Cornell, was able to do so with God's help. Her testimony was the subject of an excessive amount of discussion in our house for the ensuing week. With a heavy heart, I cried out to the Lord, wrestling in prayer on behalf of my elder son, Christopher. Out of the depths of my heart came the cry for God to show himself as a loving Father to a son whose only experience with "father" had been abandonment and neglect. I prayed for God to open the door to Harvard with full provision for my son. I do not usually pray such specific prayers unless I am absolutely certain it is God's will, but I could not help myself this time.

On Monday, I returned home from an exhausting day to discover a voicemail on our home phone from my boys' high school principal. It is common knowledge that the high school principal does not call a parent unless one's child merits such individualized attention, which is generally not good. With trepidation, I dialed the number and the principal's extension. Hearing the reluctance in my voice, she assured me this call was "good news." She then proceeded to explain that ABC News Nightline had requested she choose a student to be filmed for a piece about the college process. She had chosen my son, Christopher. This choice was based not only on his academic performance but also because of the Bread of Life food pantry ministry. I was so overwhelmed with gratitude that I could barely speak. This was answered prayer, and I could only utter the words "thank you" between sobs of gratitude.

Thus began an adventure we will not soon forget. Christopher, who tends to intellectualize and analyze everything and who feels more comfortable behind the camera than in front of one, was catapulted overnight to being the face of the college process and the spokesman for the Bread of Life. On December 5, 2015, Juju Chang and her team rode with us in the Bread of Life truck to pick up food and deliver it to a church in White Plains. This had been planned for more than a week, and we had been praying for God's favor. I prayed that God would stretch out his hand and do a miracle that could be captured on cam-

The Giving Tree

era. On the way to the food distribution point, Juju informed us of her desire to interview some of the food recipients. Pasquale and I were concerned that they would be reluctant to be filmed and may even be offended by the camera crew's presence. There is often a tremendous amount of shame associated with coming to a food pantry, mobile or otherwise.

When we arrived at the church, my heart sank. There were only a handful of people waiting outside. The usual long lines were conspicuously absent. The youth pastor informed us more people were waiting inside the church due to the cold weather. The scene unfolding before my eyes was not at all what I expected. God's priorities are not our priorities. His thoughts are not our thoughts, and his ways are not our ways. I was not present to witness Juju's initial entrance into the church or her introduction, but when I entered the building, women in tattered and stained outerwear were embracing Juju and thanking her for coming. They expressed willingness to share their stories, explaining that they "had nothing to hide." One older woman even offered Juju some coins for her parking meter to avoid a parking ticket. The incident with the coins made a lasting impression on Juju, and she repeatedly commented on it. The poor ministering to the rich and famous—who but God would imagine such a thing?

We prayed that day for the poor as we always do. If God did a miraculous physical healing that day, it was without fanfare, out of sight from people and cameras. What both the cameras and the hearts captured that day was the outpouring of love onto Juju and her team from the poor. Did we minister to the poor, or did they, with their generosity and acceptance, minister to us? They demonstrated the kingdom in both action and word. The poor, who own nothing, shared the kingdom's riches that day with Juju and the ABC News crew.

Signs, wonders, and miracles, unfortunately, do not always lead to faith. They should and do follow our ministry, for we preach a gospel of power. However, I have seen many incredible miracles, which have not resulted in faith because they are attributed to some rational cause and then forgotten. Genuine love, however, is not so easily dismissed. When there is no ulterior motive and nothing to gain, this self-sacrificing love rings true. Genuine love is the sound of the kingdom crashing

A New Song for the Bride

into the here and now. After all, the only thing that counts is faith expressing itself through love (Galatians 5:6).

On December 10, 2015, Christopher, out of the sight of the cameras, was informed of his deferral from Harvard. Heart-wrenching sobs of raw pain were released from the innermost parts of my son's soul. Years of accumulated pain from his biological father were now directed toward God. Not one word did he utter that day about Harvard—in sobs, gasps, and cries of disappointment, the anguish was all God-centered. He interpreted this "rejection" from Harvard as rejection from God. Harvard had not deemed him worthy. Therefore, God had not deemed him worthy. He repeatedly lamented, "I should have done more."

What is, indeed, the true standard of success? Is one successful because an esteemed educational institution such as Harvard declares a person "Harvard material?"

On January 16, 2016, Juju sent a note addressed Christopher and me:

> As promised—and a reminder—that there is more to life than Harvard. Thank you for sharing your lives with us. I am deeply impressed with Chris and know fundamentally that he will be a "huge success" in life regardless of which school he attends—xoxo Juju

The college admissions process continued into the spring, yielding once again a non-definitive decision from Harvard. Harvard had chosen to keep Christopher on the waitlist. On June 25, 2016, I had a dream that a large white envelope came in with an offer of admission, but Christopher would not be able to accept it because there was something "wrong" with it. On July 1, Christopher had to go to the oral surgeon to have his wisdom teeth removed. As I sat in the office waiting for him, I felt quite ill, so I kept praying, "Lord, I need this to be over. I really need the pain to end. I need Harvard to call today with an offer of admission, even if he eventually declines that offer. Not only that, Lord, but I also need the director himself to call. This way, I will know it is you."

We arrived home that day, all feeling very weary from the events of the morning. Christopher was lying on the couch when his cell phone began buzzing in his pocket. He looked at the number and picked it up. It was the Harvard Director of admissions with an offer of admission. For a moment, his face lit up. Then it fell. There was a catch—he had been put on the "z-list" of applicants who are required to take a mandatory gap year—something Christopher had never anticipated. I, on the other hand, remembered my dream. When the big white envelope from Harvard arrived, I knew he wouldn't be able to accept it. Nevertheless, he struggled with the decision for weeks, weighing every detail. Was Harvard really worth a year of his life?

One day he came into the kitchen and said to me, "Mom, I made a mistake. I thought that Harvard could tell me that I was worth something," he said, pointing to his heart, "but it can't, and it didn't." Right there and then, my son rededicated his life to Christ. Then he sent an apology to Harvard, telling them he would be unable to attend due to the gap year.

In 2020 he graduated from Yale and entered a Ph.D. program at MIT.

The college process may be over, but Christopher's story is far from finished. It is a story of what it means to be a success, not because the world declares one so, but because Father God does.

***

Value Number Two: Honor

Honor is humility in action. It is the message of the cross of Christ. Without honor, there is no harmony with heaven, for this is the attitude of heaven. The Bread of Life food pantry is located in one of the most affluent towns in the United States. The result is that the majority of volunteers are Caucasian, many are highly educated, and some are affluent. The more than twenty churches, food pantries, shelters, and soup kitchens, which comprise the food recipients, are mainly African American and Hispanic. The majority is poor, many are uneducated, and some are immigrants. We receive no salary for our work with Giving Tree, so we are forced to "sit down on the well and ask for a drink of water" from those whom we feed. This is a risky ministry model, but it is the model of the disciples who took nothing with them. We rely on the Lord's provision and on the promise that he is our shepherd. Therefore, we shall lack nothing.

A New Song for the Bride

Boaz replied, "I've been told all about what you have done for your mother-in-law since the death of your husband—how you left your father and mother and your homeland and came to live with a people you did not know before. May the Lord repay you for what you have done. May you be richly rewarded by the Lord, the God of Israel, under whose wings you have come to take refuge." (Ruth 2:11-12)

Honor is the value that has facilitated unity among the churches and has created opportunities and openness to ministry. Honor is heaven's attitude and the testimony of Jesus, which causes every knee to bow and every wall to fall. Racial divisions evaporate, ethnic lines are crossed, language barriers are eradicated, economic and educational gaps are bridged, and denominational differences are rendered inconsequential by honor, which is the attitude of Christ and the mindset of heaven.

Honor is an intentional act of humility. It is the attitude of Christ and the mindset of heaven. Honor is the value modeled by Jesus when he washed the feet of his disciples. It is the message of the cross and the attribute Jesus displayed throughout his life and ministry. Honor is the core of the servant's heart and the gospel in action. Honor knows instinctively that the way up in the kingdom of heaven is down. Honor is the purposeful placing of oneself in a position of need vis-à-vis those who the world says have nothing to offer and a place of service to those who can never repay. It goes against the grain of every aspect of our culture, which promotes self at all costs.

Honor is the antithesis of disrespect, which devalues authority in our families, schools, government, media, and even the church. Disrespect tears town the worth of another. In contrast, honor redeems and lifts its object. Honor sees the image of Jesus in one's neighbor and acknowledges it through love, time, and service. Honor upends the status quo, tearing down walls and eradicating separation lines between Samaritan and Jew, black and white, woman and man, outcast and esteemed.

The Giving Tree

***

Pasquale

Pasquale's story told in its entirety would occupy many books with untold volumes of testimonies of the countless miracles the Lord has done with him, in him, and through him. Therefore, out of sheer necessity and logistics of space, I have included only a few select excerpts of his story, all recounted in his words.

> I always wanted to do more than just say that I was a Christian; I wanted to do what the Word of God says. I believed that the gifts offered in the Bible were for everyone, so I started praying. The Word of God says if you ask, you'll receive. I searched in the Word of God, which says that everyone in the upper room was baptized in the Holy Spirit. They spoke in tongues. I found a place where I loved to pray, in a Christian cemetery with a big crucifix. Every day I would go there and pray, but nothing was happening. Then one day, I was praying in the cemetery with my eyes closed. I heard the wind coming from behind me. I opened my eyes, and there were many angels around every tombstone, so many that there seemed to be no empty space. I got scared and shut my eyes for a fraction of a second and opened them. The angels were gone. I noticed a lot of heat on my face.

> When I got home, I ran into the bathroom and washed my face. I looked up into the mirror and was surprised to see that my dark brown eyes had turned blue. That was the day I was baptized in the Holy Spirit. God touched me. I don't know why, but he touched my eyes.

> Sherri loves to share stories about how God talks to her, making me want the same thing. For weeks I kept asking the Lord, "Why not me, Lord? Why don't you speak to me?" One day she shared a story with me over the phone as I was in the car on my way to cut the grass at her house. I was jealous of how God spoke to her, so I told God, "Lord, I really want to hear from you. Speak boldly to me."

> I started to cut her grass. Suddenly, I heard the Lord tell me to shut the machine down, so I did. Then he told me to pray over the house.

> I said, "I don't have any oil, Lord." Then he manifested himself in front of me clear as day. He was on his knees as in Scripture where he was

spitting on the mud to put it on the blind man's eyes. Then he turned his head, looked at me, and said, "Use water."

I had a bottle of water in my pocket, so I began anointing the home, praying over every entrance and every door. While I was praying, the Lord showed me generational problems that were affecting the home, even before Sherri purchased it. I also saw the issues that Sherri and her family were having. The Lord was showing me all this so I would know how to pray. That was the first time I heard the Lord, right there.

The Lord calls me Joseph. That is a story as well. My mom didn't know why she gave me the name Joseph as a middle name. Nobody in my family has the name Joseph. I guess God has a great sense of humor. He named me before I was even thought of.

I'm hungry to help the Lord save the lost. I know that hell is not a nice place. I don't want to see anyone go there. I also like seeing miracles. The first miracle happened while I was in the Bronx delivering beer. I was delivering to a Bodega, a mom-and-pop deli in the Bronx. There was a man in a wheelchair sitting there with a friend. I started talking to him about Jesus. I told him that God could heal him, and I asked if I could pray for him. Then I called Sherri to partner with me in prayer over the phone while I lay hands on this man. We prayed, and then I asked him to get up out of the chair. He got up and started running around me. His friend was saying, "This can't be. He's been in this wheelchair for ten years!" Now he was running around, jumping up and down. He and his friend opened their hearts to Jesus that day.

I see a lot of miracles in the area of cancer. After God changed my eye color, I saw things I had never seen before. I often see cancer leaving a person's body at the time of the prayer. One day I was praying, and I saw cancer leave a woman's body. I looked at her and told her, "There's no more cancer. The cancer left." That was several years ago. She emailed me with her praise report. She even wrote a book and put me in it. I don't need that, but it is nice that she did:

> Pasquale, I think of you all the time and am keeping you all in my prayers. I just finished my book, *Just Three Words*, it has been a three-year labor of love God asked me to complete, and now he is opening doors. I know it will help many heal. You are in my book. I will never forget the day you prayed for

me and told me, "Karen, I saw the cancer leave your body." You have no idea how many times I held on to those empowering words when all I heard was the opposite. Words are so powerful, and yours truly helped me heal. Thank you. I went to [the hospital] a few weeks ago, and I am totally cancer free! I'm now claiming my miraculous healing for the first time. I don't need to go back for a year! Thank you so much for praying and speaking those powerful words over me. How is your family? How are you? May God bless you and lavish you with his love, and pour out his favor on you and your family.

All my love, Karen

***

Two by Two

Pasquale and I were married on December 31, 2011. According to the world's standards, we should not be together. He is a large, rough Italian with an equally hard background and a world of experience about which I have tried my best to forget. He dropped out of high school at the principal's strong suggestion because he was deemed to have no real place there and no need for education in his future. In a word, his entire life seemed to have been spent in search of trouble. On the other hand, I spent my youth in the libraries of various higher learning institutions in a vain attempt to acquire an ever-elusive sense of personal significance. There was an ocean of separation between our worlds. Apart from God, the chances our lives would ever intersect were minuscule.

One day I was introduced to him. As he glowered down at me over his broad Roman nose on the side of which a diamond was ostentatiously perched, I instantly disliked him. My thoughts about him were far from kind, including assessments of both "arrogant" and "rude." The timing of this encounter was just a brief few months after my unsolicited baptism of the Holy Spirit and my entrance into ministry. I was completely unprepared for the onslaught of spiritual warfare that came my direction, partly because I was a woman in a male-dominated church, but primarily because I had become a child of God who hears God's voice

A New Song for the Bride

and responds. My world had been upended, and life as I knew it had come to an abrupt halt. I was acutely aware of the fact that I was alone and vulnerable. One day, I prayed, "Lord, I am all alone, and this is so very difficult. I do not know if I can make this journey by myself. I will do this alone if I must, but I really would like you to send me a ministry partner."

I expected God to send me a female ministry partner. Instead, he sent me a husband I had not requested, in a package I did not want to receive. On countless occasions, I questioned whether "the God who sees" was actually "seeing" the fact that this rude, rough, uneducated man with terrible grammar that grated on my nerves was an unsuitable choice as a partner for me. I would not and could not accept this man whom God kept sending into my life. Then one day, over and above my objections, I heard the Lord tell me that Pasquale was "his best" for me.

"What?" I objected rather strenuously. "This is your best for me? We have nothing in common whatsoever. What is more, Lord, I don't even like him." Then the Lord told me to go to a church in West Haven, Connecticut, and have a man named Stephan pray for me. At the time, I was taking a class at that church. After class, I asked Stephan to pray for me. Interestingly, he told me that God had put Pasquale with me and that "he was going to adjust the yoke" because we were from very different backgrounds. To say that we were from different backgrounds was a gross understatement.

I listened as he continued to relay what the Lord was saying, but I was very skeptical and did not believe much of what was said. He began walking away from me when he abruptly spun around to face me once again and confidently declared, "And the Lord calls you Ruth, and the Naomis of the world need you." I was shocked. I had not told anyone about the new name God had given me, yet this perfect stranger knew it. "Ruth" was all I needed to hear to believe.

It has been a long journey, and the Lord is still adjusting the yoke and helping us to understand one another better. My marriage is a living lesson in honor and the kingdom of God. The world would declare that my husband, Pasquale, a high school dropout, has nothing to offer me, a Harvard-educated lawyer. In God's kingdom, however, it is the last who are first, the least are the greatest, and great faith is given to the childlike. Pasquale is a great evangelist, father, and husband. He sees more miracles of healing and salvation in one week than most Christians will see in a lifetime. He is bold, fearless, and outspoken, declaring and demonstrating the kingdom of God every day of his life all day long. I could not wish for a "better" or more "suitable" partner.

The word from God that Pasquale was "his best" for me changed my view of my husband. I now see him from heaven's perspective, which has enabled me to honor him and intentionally place myself in a position to receive from him—someone the world declares to have absolutely nothing to offer me.

***

Sam

After my powerful baptism in the Holy Spirit, I traveled to Florida to train with Francis MacNutt. There I met a man named Sam from whom I learned a great deal about the kingdom of God. Sam was blind and almost completely deaf. I would estimate his age to be mid-forties. His clothes were mismatched, with various food stains on his shirt. He immediately attracted my attention. Uncomfortable and not knowing how to interact with him, I intentionally avoided him. It would come as a great surprise later that Sam would be one of the greatest blessings to me from my time in Florida.

Sam sat in the front row, and I thought, *He must be here for healing.*

Immediately, I heard the Holy Spirit respond, *Stop judging and make a right judgment.*

What? I thought incredulously. Then I pushed the conversation quickly to the back of my mind.

Judith MacNutt stood up on the podium and held up a card with a rather lengthy opening prayer for covering written on it. "Who would like to read the opening prayer for us this morning?" she asked. To my utter amazement, Sam stood up to volunteer.

He can't even read the card, I mused. *How is he going to do the opening prayer? This is ridiculous.*

Immediately, once again, the Holy Spirit responded, *Stop judging and make a right judgment.*

What in the world is going on? I wondered. I have no idea what the Holy Spirit is referring to.

Then it happened. Sam opened his mouth to give the opening prayer, and, indeed, he did not read what was written on the card. To this day, I have never heard anyone pray the way Sam prayed. It was as if he were in heaven (maybe he was), and he prayed from that vantage point, complete with all of the sights, sounds, smells, and textures. I was instantly transported in my mind to a place of great faith and intimacy with God—all through the prayer of a blind and deaf man.

Later that same day, I asked Sam if he would do me the great honor of praying for me. He agreed without any hesitation. When he laid his hands on my head, the love and the presence of God were palpable, as was the power of God. No person who has ever prayed for me since—leaders of "great" ministries included—has ever possessed more of the anointing of God than Sam.

To the best of my knowledge, Sam was never healed by Jesus physically, perhaps because he was greater just as he was. Sam lived near a reservation of Native Americans. Initially, they considered him cursed by God, so they would pass his house and spit. Later on, however, the Lord Jesus began to do great healing miracles through Sam. Blind eyes were opened, the lame walked, the deaf heard, all in response to Sam's faith and ministry. Within months, there was a line of Native Americans outside Sam's house, not to spit, but to come for ministry and to hear the good news of Jesus Christ.

The day that Sam prayed for me, I was humbled and realized in an instant that I had everything upside down. Sam did not come to receive; in fact, I needed to receive from him because he had so much of God to give. As the power and the love of God overwhelmed me that day, I repented and acknowledged this to the Lord. I heard the Holy Spirit say, "Now, you have made a right judgment."

***

A Vision of Christ

I had the privilege of traveling to Israel with my family several years ago. During the trip, I prayed almost without ceasing. There were many great experiences, and I fell in love with the country. We were scheduled to stay in Jerusalem for four days, and I was very much looking forward to it. As I was praying, I heard the Lord say, "Look for me in Jerusalem." Those words created in me a sense of great expectation and excitement. Each day I would awaken with the thought that this day might be the day I would see a vision of the risen Christ. I looked everywhere, searched everywhere, constantly inquiring of the Holy Spirit. After four days, I had seen no vision of Jesus, had no supernatural experience, and heard only silence from the Holy Spirit. We were packing our belongings in preparation for departure, and I was praying. "Lord, I guess I didn't hear you correctly. I thought you told me I would see you in Jerusalem. I looked everywhere, but you were not here."

"Yes, I was there, Sherri."

"No, Lord, you were not," I retorted.

"I was there. You looked directly at me, but you did not see me."

"What?" I asked, confused.

Then I saw a vision of a Muslim woman with a *niqab* covering half of her face. Jesus said, "When you look at her, I want you to see me. Then you will know how I want you to treat her. Treat her as you would treat me. That is how I want you to serve me."

I have never forgotten those words or the vision of the Muslim woman. We honor Jesus by seeing the value in others. This is seeing as heaven sees (Matthew 25:31-40).

***

Value Number Three: Redemption

Over the past thirteen years, we have held fast to the mission of Christ and focused on listening to the Holy Spirit to say what he says and do what he does. This has resulted in signs, wonders, miracles, and transformation of both individual lives, churches, and entire towns. We have enjoyed favor and seen doors opened into sectors of society unimaginable for a Christian organization. Giving Tree is involved with the local public schools, businesses, the medical community, the media, and the New York State Department of Social Services.

A New Song for the Bride

We have made the conscious choice not to deviate from the simplicity of the mission of Jesus Christ. We have not crafted our own unique mission statement nor attempted a marketing or business plan. Many have declared this both reckless and unprofessional. On the contrary, we believe it is quite biblical. When Jesus appeared as a young man in the synagogue, he read his mission aloud to all in attendance—heal every wound, give victory over every bondage, and reverse every injustice. Jesus came to restore the lost glory. This was the mission of Jesus—and it is the mission of every disciple of Christ.

There is no sin so great, no tragedy so severe, no life so shattered that it cannot be restored. Nothing and no one is beyond the Lord's redemption. The book of Ruth opens with the story of three barren widows in famine-wrought Moab. The situation seems hopeless until Naomi hears that God has come to his people's aid, so Ruth and Naomi set out for a place called Bethlehem. The sound of God is present in the book of Ruth only on the lips of his people who unceasingly declare his goodness. The end of the story is redemption, a complete reversal of all of the trauma in both of their lives.

> So Boaz took Ruth and she became his wife. When he made love to her, the Lord enabled her to conceive, and she gave birth to a son. The women said to Naomi: "Praise be to the Lord, who this day has not left you without a guardian-redeemer. May he become famous throughout Israel! He will renew your life and sustain you in your old age. For your daughter-in-law, who loves you and who is better to you than seven sons, has given him birth." (Ruth 4:13-16)

In one form or another, every human being asks the question, "For what purpose am I here?" The quest for meaning and significance is the driving force behind the accumulation of wealth, power, possessions, and prestige. It is the unquenchable force behind competition, performance, striving, and even religion. Religion's response to the question of significance is the world's value system where "more" is better, and a rise to the "top" is equivalent to importance. In contrast, purpose in the kingdom of God is inextricably intertwined with what it means to be a child of God. A child of God is a child of faith, a child who worships the Father in Spirit and in truth. A child of God is one who hears the voice of God and responds appropriately. Every person—without exception—was created to release the glory of God—*to be sounded*. This is "Christ in you, the hope of glory."

***

Restoring the Glory

Perhaps the greatest miracle I have ever witnessed occurred in the fall of 2008. Pasquale and I had been invited to conduct a healing service in a Korean church in New Jersey. We requested that the pastor send us a list of the most seriously ill congregants one week before the service to begin our intercession for the sick. When we arrived, the pastor handed us a new list. At the top of this list, a name was penciled in, which was illegible. The list was quite long, so we promised to stay until everyone had the opportunity to receive ministry.

I took the list and was about to begin quite logically with the first name, which was penciled in at the top, but I hesitated, however, for I sensed that the Holy Spirit wanted a specific order for ministry. Intellectually, this made no sense to me, and I questioned it to myself. I decided, however, to override my own internal objections and call the people according to the leading of the Holy Spirit. The night was filled with extraordinary healing miracles. Blind eyes were opened, limbs were healed, and many more miracles occurred. As the evening progressed into night, we became increasingly tired, and our strength was finished. After hours of ministry, finally, there was only one name remaining on the list. This was the name that was penciled in at the top.

Two people ushered the woman forward. My heart sank, as did my faith. I was exhausted, and my eyes beheld a woman whose body was riddled with such extensive damage that her condition immediately brought about a sense of hopelessness despite all of the miracles we had just witnessed. The severe pain and dizziness she was experiencing prevented her from standing, so ushers helped her lie down on the

A New Song for the Bride

floor in order for us to minister. Her chin and the back of her skull had both been crushed in a car accident four years earlier. There was a metal plate on the back of her head, and drainage tubes flanked both sides of her face. I was utterly spent. Inwardly I questioned the Lord, "Why did you choose to save this one for last? She has more than everyone else combined. I am so tired. I have nothing left," I objected.

Pasquale placed his hands gently underneath the back of her skull. I bent down over the top of her as she was lying there on the floor. I delicately put my hands on each side of her face and uttered the only words that came to my mind, "In the name of Jesus, let the trauma be reversed." Immediately, I felt the bones in her jaw move beneath my hands. I was shocked and looked up at Pasquale, whose expression conveyed he was sensing the same movement in the back of her skull. We remained in that position as the movement continued for a few minutes. Then I felt the Holy Spirit draw me away from her. We stood next to the pastor for what seemed an eternity but was, in reality, not more than fifteen or twenty minutes. The pastor glanced over at me and inquired as to what was happening. My response was that Jesus was in the house.

When the woman arose from the floor, all mouths dropped open in shock, including my own. She was completely transformed. Her face was round and perfect, and she was radiating joy. We were all overwhelmed at the blessing of witnessing such an amazing miracle. Curiosity prompted me to ask her to describe her experience. She explained that she had been in extreme pain for hours while waiting for her turn to receive ministry. She had been praying for others, but the only prayer she was able to pray for herself was, "Jesus, let the trauma be reversed."

When I said those words, the pain began to be released from her body, starting with her eyes. The extensive nerve damage caused by the accident had been a constant source of pain throughout her body for four years. Relief from the nerve pain began in her eyes, and then the relief traveled throughout the rest of her body. She told us that there was a figure in blinding white light standing by my right side while I was praying. When I stepped back, the figure stepped forward. She knew it was Jesus.

The trauma was reversed in this woman's body, and healing was brought to her soul in the name of Jesus. Although I didn't realize it at the time, the statement "let the trauma be reversed" is a heartfelt cry for Jesus to restore the glory. This is the promise of Isaiah 61. It was the mission of Jesus, and it is the purpose of every disciple of Jesus Christ.

***

Margie

Margie stepped forward to take her turn in the prayer line. She was severely bent over, almost achieving an upside-down "U" shape, and walked with a cane on one side and the assistance of a friend on the other. The friend had encouraged her to come forward. Margie had suffered from arthritis from the age of six and had endured pain and the inability to walk on her own for the entirety of her adult life. I bent down to look into her eyes and listened for the Holy Spirit who whispered the word *identity*. Identity? I had no idea what he was referring to. I began to gently ask Margie some questions. Margie declared emphatically, "I know that God has given me this affliction to teach me something and because I am strong enough to carry it. He never gives us more than what we can handle."

I asked her, "Do you believe that God the Father loves you?"

"Yes," said Margie.

"Do you believe that he loves you and wants the best for you?"

"Yes," said Margie.

"Do you believe that a loving father who wants the best for his child would want to give his child sickness as a gift?"

"No," said Margie.

"Then why would God, who loves you beyond limit and wants the best for you, give you sickness as a gift?"

"He wouldn't. That doesn't make sense," said Margie.

"No, it doesn't make sense. Now what do you believe about your arthritis?"

"God did not give it to me," declared Margie.

"Do you believe that God, who loves you, wants you to be free from this debilitating disease?"

"Yes," said Margie.

The prayer for Margie was a simple one and took about two minutes. I simply declared her healed in the name of Jesus. She finally straightened up her spine after more than thirty years, tossed her cane to her friend, and marched triumphantly out of the sanctuary.

***

Raising the Dead

There are times when we are the proverbial "last resort." In other words, if all else has failed, what does one have to lose in risking that God might actually still heal today? I believe this was the case when a pastor from New Jersey called and asked whether we would be willing to pray for a woman with cancer who was told she would be dead in a matter of days. Pasquale and I went to the hospital to pray for her. She was lying in bed, and her body, particularly her abdominal area, was completely distended and disfigured by tumors. When we arrived, two people were in the room, an elderly man and woman. Neither of them spoke English, so we had no information regarding their relationship to the dying woman.

As we began to pray, the Holy Spirit spoke of a promise this woman had made to him some time ago. She was very weak, but still able to speak, so I inquired whether she remembered making a promise to God. She nodded her head sadly and said, "Yes, I promised him years ago that I would live my life as his child, but I never kept that promise."

"Would you like a chance to keep it?" I asked.

"I would give anything to be able to keep it," she said.

"I believe you are going to get a second chance," I answered.

As we prayed, the elderly man began to weep softly. Neither of the couple said a word, but remained utterly silent throughout the prayer. There were no trumpet blasts, no fanfare, just the peaceful presence of the Holy Spirit in that hospital room. Pasquale and I left, not knowing what God had done.

The Giving Tree

It was not until several months later when the pastor informed us that all of the tumors had completely disappeared and the woman was now back in her home raising her three young children. More than that, the elderly man who wept while we prayed was her father from whom she had been estranged for years prior to that day. They forgave each other and their relationship was completely restored.

***

Pastor Rick

When God is doing miracles, word tends to travel. People come from near and far to receive the Lord's healing. Such was the case with Pastor Rick. Rick was a pastor from the Bronx who suffered a stroke and was paralyzed from the neck down. His daughter contacted us to inquire whether we would be willing to drive to Queens and pray for him in the nursing home where he was staying. That week we went to see Pastor Rick, who was eagerly waiting for us in his room.

Covering his room walls were Scriptures, quotes from Jesus, and articles that were evidence of a man of faith. He was sitting with his back toward us as we entered. He turned his wheelchair around quickly and greeted us with a broad smile. I leaned over him as we began to pray and saw a clear picture of him walking around the streets of the Bronx, completely healed. I said, "Pastor Rick, Jesus is going to heal you today. Do you believe that?"

"Amen," he said. "I believe Jesus is going to heal me."

I don't remember the remainder of the details of the very brief prayer we prayed. The atmosphere was one of faith, joy, and expectation. It felt like a celebration! Pasquale and I hugged him and left Pastor Rick just as we had found him—in a wheelchair.

The next week we called the nursing home and inquired about the wellbeing of Pastor Rick. "He is not here any longer," the receptionist informed us.

"What do you mean, he is not there? Was he transferred somewhere?" I asked.

"No," the receptionist replied simply. "The day after you two came and prayed for him, he got up and walked out of here."

I remembered the picture I had of him walking around in the Bronx and smiled, knowing that God had done what he promised.

***

Ralph

On our trips to Vermont, we always stop to see a friend who owns a barbershop in the area. She prays for her customers and allows us to do likewise. On this particular day, Pasquale and I prayed for a few people who were getting their hair cut. One of them was a man named Ralph who was suffering from liver cancer. His face was drawn and pale. He was very thin, and his hair was mostly gray. He had an upcoming doctor's appointment in a few days. We prayed that the cancer would leave his body and blessed him with health in the name of Jesus. He thanked us. We said our good-byes and left the shop.

Approximately a year passed when we saw our friend again. She told us that several months after the prayer, Ralph returned for a haircut. He was scarcely recognizable. He appeared ten years younger—vibrant, healthy, and with a full head of dark hair. He told her that there were no traces of cancer in his body when he went to the doctor. Both he and the doctors were baffled. He just shook his head and said, "It must have been the prayer that day in your shop."

***

Nora

As was the case with the centurion in the days of Jesus (Matthew 8:5-13), there is no distance in the spiritual realm. There have been numerous cases of healings over the phone and the Internet where the words spoken were at a significant geographical distance from the prayer recipient. One of these involved Nora. One morning Nora, an acquaintance from North Dakota, called to ask for prayer. She was very ill, and her doctors were in a quandary as to both the source of the problem and the proper treatment. Her thyroid gland had inexplicably and suddenly stopped functioning. Consequently, she had been bedridden for weeks and was on the verge of losing her job.

The Giving Tree

I offered to pray for her. I heard the Holy Spirit say the word *fear*.

I asked her, "Nora, are you afraid of anything?"

"No," she answered quickly.

Puzzled, I continued to pray and listen. Again I heard the word *fear* and asked, "Nora, do you have any anxiety?"

"Oh, yes!" she responded. "I really struggle with anxiety most of the time."

"Well, anxiety is just another word for fear," I explained. "Fear is at odds with faith. You have allowed fear into your life."

I explained to Nora that fear is a sin, and I led her in a prayer of repentance for allowing fear into her life. Then I commanded the spirit of fear to leave her in the name of Jesus and released peace into her life and over her thyroid gland. Nora phoned about a week later to tell me that she had been completely healed. Her thyroid was functioning normally, and the doctors were asking what had happened. Nora told them Jesus heals! She then bought a ticket to New York to show me her good health in person.

***

Yale University

As my husband and I walked the sprawling campus of Yale University, the command the Lord had given us to "take back what is his" seemed more than daunting. It seemed impossible. "Lord, where do we even begin?" I questioned the Holy Spirit.

"Begin with the heart," I heard him say.

"The heart? It doesn't have a heart," I protested. "It's a school. A school doesn't have a heart." The Holy Spirit insisted otherwise. I remember reasoning that if Yale were a person, the heart would be the oldest part, the part which would have been formed first. My husband and I set out to the oldest part of campus. Then we saw it, right there on the New Haven Green, a church right in the middle with a sign that read, "Christ-centered in the heart of New Haven." It had a large heart right next to an inscription that explained how New Haven was started with open-air worship on the Green.

A New Song for the Bride

For four years, my husband and I traveled to Yale monthly to pray over the buildings, the student body, and the faculty, all the while reclaiming the legacy of God's truth and light that had once been so strong there. From the outset, the Holy Spirit told me to see what he sees and speak that destiny over Yale. There was always a serious disconnect between what I saw with my physical eyes and what the Holy Spirit was saying. Every time I would step onto that campus, the Holy Spirit would seem to start singing and rejoicing within me. I have rarely felt such joy.

On February 27, 2020, the week before the Coronavirus outbreak in New York, some friends and I went up to Yale for the Collegiate Day of Prayer to pray for revival in the universities. That fact alone that the leadership had chosen Yale to host the event and that Yale had agreed was already a sign to me that the Lord was, indeed, taking Yale back as he had promised. When I witnessed the students with humble hearts crying out to the Lord for their school, for their friends, and even for their professors who had tried to teach them not to believe, I was deeply affected. "This is it," I thought. "This is the beginning of the revival. Surely, God has heard their prayers and ours."

"This used to be a Godless place when I went here," a Yale alumnus told me. He had just celebrated his 50th reunion the week prior in the very chapel where we were now standing. "It no longer is," he declared with tears in his eyes.

The wells of revival run deep at Yale, for it has a long history not only of educating men (and women) in the truth of God's Word, but also of Holy Spirit outpourings which have radically transformed lives. At present, the New Haven Green shows little of its former glory, frequented now by drug addicts and drug dealers. From Heaven's perspective, it seems like the perfect place for a revival right in the heart of New Haven—where it all began with worship on the Green.

***

Value Number Four: Faith

To be a disciple of Christ is synonymous with being a witness for Christ. At the very center of the Christian journey and at the heart of discipleship lies the issue of faith. Somehow we as the church have been

The Giving Tree

lulled into complacency concerning the nature of biblical faith. Faith has become optional, accessible in its fullness only to the elite few, the so-called "generals" in God's army. We have compromised with our own lack of it and have opted out of it as a necessity for being in Christ. Nominal Christianity sweeps aside faith as a luxury one can ill-afford, as faith tends to call people out of their comfort zone. Discipleship is not a program or a curriculum. It cannot be learned or acquired in a day, in a week, or even a year. One cannot grasp all of its implications in the course of a retreat or a conference. Discipleship is a lifestyle, both in and outside of the community of like-minded believers, which has a melody, as it were, a common thread of sound, and that sound is the sound of faith expressing itself through love.

The major emphasis of Giving Tree, and the target it is squarely aimed at, is the issue of faith. All of the trials, testimonies, and years of experience have concluded in unison that faith is, was, and always has been the primary requirement for the child of God. Jesus sent his disciples out to proclaim the kingdom, heal the sick, and drive out demons. He sent them out on an impossible mission and instructed them to take nothing with them. The only provision they carried with them was his presence. It was the presence of Jesus Christ through the Holy Spirit that ensured the impossible would become possible. This is the essence of faith. It is the sound of what it means to "live not by bread alone but on every word that comes from the mouth of God." Nominal Christianity declares faith optional. Biblical Christianity states otherwise.

How does one judge whether one is a success in the eyes of God? What is the measurement by which to assess not only individuals but also ministries and churches? The tendency in the American church is to measure success in worldly terms in which quantity is everything. The greater the number of people gathered, the more lucrative the offering, the higher the podium, the louder and more flamboyant the worship team, the more successful the church or ministry is deemed. In stark contrast, success in God's kingdom is not defined in terms of quantity or size, but rather in terms of faith, for without faith, it is impossible to please God (Hebrews 11:6). Faith, in turn, is measured by obedience: "Hearing the word of God and responding appropriately." In these terms—and only in these terms—can the ministry of the obedient prophet Jeremiah, to whom not one person responded, be deemed a "success."

***

Results

I remember the exact moment in my journey with Jesus when everything changed. From the moment I was baptized in the Holy Spirit, set on my feet, and sent out to pray, signs, wonder, and miracles followed everywhere. The signs and wonders seemed to come so easily that somewhere deep inside of me, I began to think somehow that they depended on me. One evening at the Saturday night service during which we did altar calls for healing, I spotted a man in a wheelchair making his way straight down the aisle. I earnestly prayed that he would make a beeline for some other prayer minister. When I opened my eyes, undeterred by my prayers, he was rolling his way right down the aisle toward me. He came to a complete stop and looked up at me expectantly. He declared that he had been paralyzed for ten years and wanted to walk again. The paralyzed man believed in the healing power of Jesus. If there was a problem in this situation, it was clearly with me.

Silently, I was praying, *Jesus, help my unbelief.*

After inquiring how he became paralyzed and listening to the Holy Spirit, I began to pray. A few minutes passed. He felt nothing. I prayed harder. Still, he felt nothing. I leaned in over him farther and prayed with even more intensity. I felt drops of sweat trickling down the middle of my back. He felt nothing. Suddenly I heard the Holy Spirit say, "Sherri, you cannot will me to heal." That day marked a turning point in my journey with God. It was both humbling and humiliating to think I could twist God's arm to make him heal. Now I know that my job and my only part to play in the healing process is to love the person in front of me. The healing is all up to God. This is a partnership in which the yoke is easy, and the burden is light.

As I prayed from that place of rest, the paralyzed man rose to his feet and stood that night for the first time in ten years. With tears streaming down his face, he praised the Lord Jesus, to whom belong all of the honor, glory, and praise.

***

The Choice

One evening I was sitting in the pew as the pastor droned on about a subject I had long forgotten. However, what was forever etched into my memory was how I heard the voice of the Holy Spirit speak so clearly amid that message. *I need you to do three things.*

Okay, I answered. Then he began to list them one by one. I responded rapidly to the first two with, *Yes, Lord*. I had quickly assented to them because, quite frankly, they were easy. The third request, however, made me pause. He said, *I want you to go over and command John to walk in the name of Jesus.*

What? I thought. Immediately a battle began taking shape on my mind. *I can't do that. The people in this church do not even believe that God heals today.* The objections piled up one after another. *John is in the front of the church, Lord. I am going to look like a fool.*

Clearly, the Holy Spirit spoke again. *Every choice is a choice between fear and faith; which will you choose?* The fog cleared from my brain as I understood that to have faith is to obey against all odds. After the sermon ended, I got up from my seat and walked over to John, a rather large twenty-three-year-old autistic man who could not walk. I had prayed for him many times before, but this time would be different. I looked at him as directly as I could and said, "John, in the name of Jesus, get up and walk." He thought we were playing a game, so I took him by the hand and pulled up into an upright position. He flung his long arm over my shoulders. I glanced up to see that we were now the single focus of attention in a church that did not believe in healing, miracles, or in any gifts of the Holy Spirit, for that matter. A further complication was the fact that I was a woman, and women did not occupy visible ministry positions in this church.

Mouths dropped open as they watched me (5'1") parade up and down along the front pew with John (approximately 5'7") draped over me. "John is going to walk in the name of Jesus. Jesus is healing him," I declared to the unbelieving crowd. In fact, John not only walked that day, but he also ran. He ran right out to the parking lot, and we had to run after him to catch him. A sign, a wonder, a miracle happened that day right in front of a packed crowd. The tragic part of the story is that, like the Pharisees of Jesus' day, they still did not believe.

***

Heidi

It was November 2015 at the food pantry where we distribute food and offer prayer. Understandably, the most frequent prayer need at the food pantry is for financial provision, followed by prayers for physical healing and healing for families. One woman stepped up eagerly for prayer. When I inquired as to what she would like from Jesus, she replied quite simply, "I need more of him. If I have more of him, then I have all I need. I have problems, but he is the solution to them all." Heidi was the first person I had encountered who instinctively knew that God is enough. I quickly explained to her about the baptism of the Holy Spirit and how we can all hear God. Then I asked her if that is what she wanted. She said yes emphatically.

This was just the beginning of my acquaintance with Heidi. She showed up about a month later at the women's prayer group I host at my home. She had spent the last four weeks sitting at the feet of Jesus, soaking in his presence, and learning Scripture through the Holy Spirit, and she showed me a notebook full of notes from this time. There was another woman in the group, Carolina, a simple boisterous no-nonsense woman with only a high school education. Up to this point, Carolina would stand in silence with her head bowed while the rest of the group would pray. She emphatically insisted that she would not, could not, and did not know how to pray.

This day would mark a turning point for both Carolina and Heidi. As we began the prayer, Carolina started shaking her hands, saying that they felt like they were on fire. We explained that this was God choosing to use her to heal someone. Heidi needed physical healing, as she had recently battled breast cancer. Carolina placed her hands on Heidi and prayed for her to be healed and set free. She spoke healing and freedom over her in the name of Jesus. Heidi said that she had walked in with a migraine headache, but it disappeared during the prayer. In the course of ten to fifteen minutes, Heidi's pain was gone, and Carolina had been catapulted from the spectator seat in the Christian journey to the starring role.

***

Jesus is Enough

The line for prayer was very long that evening. I had seven prayer ministers on the prayer team at that time, but even that was not enough. Word of the miracles God was doing has gotten out, and people were lining up for prayer. It was and continues to be my view that God can work miracles through any believer at any time due to the indwelling of the Holy Spirit. Therefore, I strongly discouraged people from preferring prayer from me instead of from members of my team. However, on this particular evening, one woman created quite a stir and was disrupting the prayer line.

She made her way around all of the prayer ministers and, pointing directly at me, declared in no uncertain terms, "I want her to pray for me." I assured her that any of the ministers could pray for her and instructed her to get back into line and wait her turn. She became even more adamant and refused to move. In fact, she assumed an aggressive posture directly in front of me. Arms crossed, she stared defiantly right at me, and the standoff was now the focus of everyone's attention.

I was very tired from the previous ministry, and it was getting quite late. I had run out of patience but was concerned about the other people who were waiting their turn. "Fine," I will pray for you, I said reluctantly. As I glanced at her, I knew this woman was extremely broken, but I had no idea what to do for her. I knew, however, that Jesus did, so I said, "Jesus, this one is all yours."

What happened then is difficult to capture in words. The light of glory came out of heaven on her. Her face began to change. Her posture relaxed, and it was as if an invisible burden was lifted from her shoulders. Her face lit up with joy, and she began to smile. Her appearance was glowing. Once again, she captured everyone's attention, but for a very different reason. She was shining with the Lord's glory and was completely transformed in a matter of minutes.

One of the other prayer ministers came up to me. "What in the world did you do to her? She left a completely different person."

I answered simply, "I didn't know what to do. I didn't even want to pray for her, so I gave her to Jesus. He did the rest."

***

Daniel

I really enjoy praying for people who are involved in the New Age or the occult. These are times when Jesus tends to announce himself in amazing ways. This particular day was no exception. Daniel was a therapist in Vermont who used New Age approaches for healing, e.g., energy healing, Reiki, etc. However, Daniel had some health issues of his own which would not respond to any of the treatments he was using for his clients. His wife called me on this particular day and inquired whether I would come and pray for him. Both Daniel and his wife had been educated in Catholic schools and had negative experiences, so they turned away from God.

The prayer for Daniel was a simple one. I did not touch him. In fact, there remained a healthy distance of about three feet between us throughout the prayer. I felt that the Holy Spirit wanted Daniel to know what he was experiencing had nothing to do with me. He stood in silence as I prayed for him to know the love of God and who God really is. I left after about an hour, once again not knowing what God had done.

About six months later, I returned to Vermont. Daniel contacted me and said, "I want what you have."

"I am not sure to what you are referring," I answered, somewhat confused by this statement.

"After you prayed for me, whatever you have, that peace, that light, stayed with me for three days," said Daniel. "It was the most amazing thing I have ever experienced. That is why I want what you have."

"Daniel, it's not what I have, but whom I have. That was Jesus. I have Jesus in my heart and in my life. It is he who does the work through me. I left, but he stayed. You need Jesus. Jesus is whom you want, and if you accept him in your heart, he will never leave," I explained.

The Giving Tree

Daniel did not accept Jesus that day, but I believe that one day he will. Daniel refers all of his "hard cases" to me, like cancer and other "terminal" illnesses. This is a bit odd, but even at this point, he recognizes that the one whom I serve is greater than the one he serves.

***

Doris

We were called to pray for a diabetic woman who was in the hospital to have both of her legs amputated due to poor circulation. When Pasquale and I arrived, she was lying in her hospital bed, and both of her legs from the knee down were a bluish color. As we began to pray, I laid my hands on her right leg, which was cold to the touch. We commanded the circulation to be restored and the normal blood flow to be returned to her legs in the name of Jesus as the Holy Spirit led us to pray. While we prayed for both legs, I prayed more for the right leg and saw that the flesh began to turn a rosy pink color, and the warmth began to return to her calf area. We ministered to her for about thirty minutes, said our good-byes, and left.

Through the word of some friends, we heard the next day that the surgery had continued as planned and the amputation had been completed. My heart sank. I thought I had witnessed Jesus heal her legs, and I was disappointed for her and confused as to the apparent outcome. Doubt crept into my mind, and I wondered whether I imagined the manifestations of healing I had seen.

A few weeks later, however, we went to see her. She was radiating with joy. "God answered my prayer," she explained. "I prayed that they would save my right leg so I could drive. When they went to operate, the doctors found the circulation restored to the right leg. They took only my left one. I can still drive!" She exclaimed with excitement.

I was stunned. From my perspective, this prayer had been a failure, but there was a detail about which I had been completely unaware—her desire for her right leg to be saved so she could drive. To Doris, this was an answer to prayer.

***

A New Song for the Bride

Marion

We had driven up to Vermont for Christmas 2014. I had no plans to travel that year and, frankly, no desire. However, a young man who was about to enter the Marines contacted us with his wish to be baptized before his induction. At the same time, a member of our team traveled to Vermont to collect testimonies of God's financial provision and invited him to join a group of young people. Pasquale and I felt the Lord leading us to agree to meet them in Vermont to do the baptism there. We have no access to facilities in Vermont, so we agreed that we would do the baptism in Lake Champlain, regardless of the temperature. The trip was filled with blessings, prayers, and baptism on Christmas Eve in the freezing rain in front of a crowd of witnesses singing Christmas carols and capturing the moment on their smartphones.

On Christmas Day, I wanted to rest and spend some time with the Lord while cross-country skiing, so I bought a day ski pass. My older son, Christopher, immediately took issue with my expenditure of $25 for the pass. His view was that we had no salary and were trying to save money, so why would I spend money on something so frivolous when I was praying for financial blessings. To him, it made no sense. I started on my ski adventure in a poor state of mind. Feeling very guilty for spending money on the ski pass after my conversation with my son, I began to pray. "Lord, I don't understand. I believe that you want your servants to have rest. You want us to have a vacation. We need rest. I am feeling so tired. Anyway, if you want us to have a vacation, could you please provide one and show my son that you want us to rest?"

The Holy Spirit spoke to me and told me to go to the chapel. Now the chapel on this particular trail is on the top of a very steep hill. To get there, I would not be able to ski but would have to climb. I needed rest, not more work, so I began to object. "Lord, I am tired and do not want to climb up to the chapel. I want to ski." Repeatedly, he told me to go to the chapel.

After more objections on my part, he said, "Go the back way."

Now I had never taken the back path to the chapel, but I decided to take a chance and try. It was much easier and flatter than the more familiar front path to the chapel. I arrived at the top of the hill to see a woman ascending the other side. We met in front of the chapel. "Nice view," I said. "I like it up here," I remarked in an attempt to strike up a conversation.

"Yes, normally I like it up here," she responded, "but I have to snowshoe today while my husband is skiing. I cannot ski with him because a boat motor crushed my foot, and I have pain in my foot."

I told her I was a Christian minister and offered to pray for her foot. She accepted graciously, and the pain left. Then she said, "I am in ministry too, but it is an unusual ministry. My husband and I own a villa on Antigua and we offer it to ministers and missionaries to use for vacation. We know that being in ministry is difficult, and God wants them to be able to rest."

I was shocked. When I told her about the conversation with my son and my prayer, we both laughed—another answered prayer. In August 2015, my family and I traveled to Antigua for almost two weeks of rest, thanks to both God and Marion. More than that, before we left, I received this email from her. I did not know about her condition when we prayed in the chapel, but God is faithful.

Hi Sherri,

I loved seeing your recent pictures of your outreach. So fun to see you minister to Rosemarie Von Trapp since that is where we were connected. I do not know if I told you, but just before meeting you, I found out that I had a 7mm lump in my left breast and possible stage 2 given my family history. After several more high-definition ultrasounds and continued tests, the physician called me in to actually show me the pictures of my left breast and the lump and now the unexplained absence of it! The Great Physician at work again. Thanks for all you are doing and all the ways you are ministering to the body of Christ.

Grace,

Marion

***

A New Song for the Bride

Sandy

A few months after I was baptized in the Holy Spirit, set on my feet, sent out to pray for healing, and distinctly before I was equipped and prepared, a woman named Sandy came for ministry. Ostensibly, she had come for help with some issues with unforgiveness. I asked the standard questions about occult involvement before we began what I had assumed would be a quick ministry session. At this time, I had no experience in deliverance. I invited the Holy Spirit to come, and in seconds I was flat on my back with Sandy, a rather large woman, on top of me. I was literally pinned to the floor. I had two prayer ministers with me in the room, both of them as inexperienced as I.

I managed to extract myself from underneath Sandy to find one of the prayer ministers in tears and the other petrified with fear. At this point, Sandy began slithering across the floor on her back in a snakelike fashion. She spoke to me in a male voice, saying, "We are leaving."

"You are correct on one point," I responded. "You are leaving. Sandy, however, is staying."

I had no idea what I was doing, but I knew that Jesus was in the room and that he knew exactly how to deal with this. I asked one prayer minister to pray and the other to read Scripture out loud. I took authority over Sandy in the name of Jesus, forbade interference from any demons, and silenced them in the name of Jesus. As it turned out, Sandy was not honest with me regarding her occult involvement. She had been deeply involved in witchcraft and divination. It took over two hours for her to be set free. Sandy stood behind me in the worship service that evening, her face covered in the glory of God. She was set free not because I knew what I was doing. In fact, I did not. She was set free because I had faith in Jesus, listened to him, and did what he told me to do.

A Triumphant Legacy

For Ruth of the Bible and for this modern-day Ruth, the overarching question has been, "What if God does not come for me?" Yet, throughout, the voice of faith has protested, "But what if he does?"

The Giving Tree

> Then Naomi took the child in her arms and cared for him. The women living there said, "Naomi has a son!" And they named him Obed. He was the father of Jesse, the father of David. (Ruth 4:16-17)

Ruth was a parable of what it means to be a child of God, living a life of obedience that comes from faith. She clung to God, trusted, sacrificed, and loved all with the passionate commitment that declares "God is enough." Faith is the attribute that earned Ruth the Moabitess, a place, not only in the Bible but also in David and Jesus's lineage. Ruth left a legacy of children of God, children of faith, who hear God and respond in obedience. They hear God, see as he sees, and say what he says. The sound of faith is the sound of heaven, the orchestra on earth, and the symphony of believers. The Holy Spirit combined with faith is the "Christ in you, the hope of glory," the potential of "being sounded," of releasing God's power on earth through the spoken word:

> To proclaim the year of the Lord's favor and the day of vengeance of our God, to comfort all who mourn, and provide for those who grieve in Zion—to bestow on them a crown of beauty instead of ashes, the oil of joy instead of mourning, and a garment of praise instead of a spirit of despair. They will be called oaks of righteousness, a planting of the Lord for the display of his splendor. (Isaiah 61:2-3)

Epilogue

"Don't you want your money?" the New York State Supreme Court judge bellowed down at me impatiently from the bench. Money was most definitely not what I wanted. Money was simply not enough. How does one quantify all of the pain, loss, and years in money? With the full knowledge that he could do nothing that would satisfy my request, I nevertheless opened my mouth to utter my heart's cry, "I want justice, your Honor."

Twelve years had passed since my unsolicited baptism of the Holy Spirit and my induction into the ranks of the children of God. Everything had come full circle, and I found myself once again in the courtroom. My ex-husband, who had disappeared for over a decade into Russia, had announced his return with the service of legal papers. Having cried out to God for justice on behalf of my children and myself for years, I found myself in the very place I had hoped to avoid—another courtroom battle. At the first of what would later seem like endless appearances before the court, she stated casually that my response papers had somehow been misplaced. Still, we were nonetheless to begin oral arguments immediately. Bolstered with confidence by the advantageous state of affairs, my ex-husband's attorney began presenting his case.

Seemingly eager to clear the docket and move the matter along, the court agreed with his reasoning and seemed irritated that I should object. The unexpected turn of events had left me at a loss, and I finally heard myself say, "Your honor, I have no idea why I am even here."

The Giving Tree

Having now gotten her attention, she focused squarely on me as she asked, "What do you mean?"

It was at that point that I knew this time would be different. It would be different because I was different.

After numerous courtroom appearances, I was offered a settlement, the terms of which would release all of my ex-husband's past debts owed on behalf of the children and all future debts and obligations as well. This was certainly not the outcome for which I had hoped, and it was definitely not the justice I sought. Against all reason, the Holy Spirit led me to accept the offer. My ex-husband had brought me into the courtroom, and I had given him what he wanted—freedom.

All ties to the past had been severed with complete finality. I had been waiting so long for a resolution that I did not recognize it when it came. It looked and felt like defeat. Blank faces stared back at me as I announced my decision to settle to my friends and family. They didn't have to say a word as I could read it on their faces, "God did not come for you." For months I was numb, wondering whether I had done what was right. People accused me of giving away the child support, which belonged to my children. I began to question every moment, every word that was said in the courtroom. Only time would tell whether I had indeed heard God.

***

"Do you, Sir, take Zachary to be your son?" the Family Court judge inquired of my new husband as she smiled at us from her bench. The wall to my left was lined with unfamiliar people; mostly court employees gathered to witness a noteworthy event—the adoption of two young men, one nineteen, the other twenty years old.

"It is not often," explained the judge, "that there is a cause for celebration in my courtroom. Today is a very special day."

Epilogue

Adoption, many mistakenly believe, is somehow inferior, second-rate, or second best. This is a misconception, which could not be further from the truth. In the book of Romans, Paul uses the metaphor of Roman adoption to symbolize a believer's relationship with the Father:

> The Spirit you received does not make you slaves, so that you live in fear again; rather, the Spirit you received brought about your adoption to sonship. And by him we cry, "Abba, Father." (Romans 8:15)

In Roman culture, the father had the power to decide whether a child born into the family would remain or be disowned for a variety of reasons. Therefore, the relationship was not necessarily either desired or even permanent. In the case of adoption, however, the situation was entirely different. First, the adoptee, who was usually an adult, was both desired and freely chosen by the parents. Second, he (in rarer cases "she") became a permanent member of the family and could not be disowned.

The Family Court Judge continued, now addressing my sons, "Christopher John, do you agree to accept Pasquale Falco to be your father?" She seemed to be in absolutely no hurry as she deliberately emphasized each word in the sentence. The gallery of onlookers had pulled out tissues as the whole process had brought tears to their eyes. As I watched my sons hug their new father, I suddenly understood God's justice, for I was witnessing it in living color.

As we were planning the adoption and filling out all of the paperwork, many voices questioned us. "What difference does it make?" they argued, "Your boys are adults."

That day made all of the difference, not just for my sons but also for me. I walked out of the courtroom for the final time, completely free. God came for me that day, and my heart was healed as I watched my sons as they heard their new father say, "I choose you."

About the Author

Sherri Falco and her husband, Pasquale, co-founded Giving Tree Global, a marketplace ministry whose goal is to demonstrate the love of Jesus Christ in a tangible way. She is a Harvard-educated lawyer, with an MBA in international business, an MA in Slavic linguistics, and a BA in Russian and in economics. She also holds a doctorate degree from United Theological Seminary. Sherri has international business experience as finance manager for Procter & Gamble Germany, and was a key member of the start-up team of Procter & Gamble Russia. Her legal experience comes from her time spent as an associate at Simpson Thatcher and Bartlett in New York City. Sherri currently teaches discipleship and spiritual formation at Global Awakening Theological Seminary, and greatly enjoys helping others grow in their relationship with Christ.

Sherri can be contacted at sherri@givingtreeglobal.org

www.ingramcontent.com/pod-product-compliance
Lightning Source LLC
Chambersburg PA
CBHW071825080526
44589CB00012B/921